Global Entrepreneurship Monitor India Report 2019/20

A National Study on Entrepreneurship

Authored by

Sunil Shukla
Director-General Entrepreneurship Development Institute of India

Pankaj Bharti
Assistant Professor, Entrepreneurship Development Institute of India

Amit Kumar Dwivedi
Associate Professor, Entrepreneurship Development Institute of India

T0383137

Routledge
Taylor & Francis Group

LONDON AND NEW YORK

First published 2021
by CRC Press
2 Park Square, Milton Park, Abingdon, Oxon, OX14 4RN

and by Routledge
52 Vanderbilt Avenue, New York, NY 10017

© 2021 Sunil Shukla et.al.

Routledge is an imprint of the Taylor & Francis Group, an informa business

The right of Sunil Shukla et.al. to be identified as author[/s] of this work has been asserted by them in accordance with sections 77 and 78 of the Copyright, Designs and Patents Act 1988.

Reasonable efforts have been made to publish reliable data and information, but the author and publisher cannot assume responsibility for the validity of all materials or the consequences of their use. The authors and publishers have attempted to trace the copyright holders of all material reproduced in this publication and apologize to copyright holders if permission to publish in this form has not been obtained. If any copyright material has not been acknowledged please write and let us know so we may rectify in any future reprint.

All rights reserved. No part of this book may be reprinted or reproduced or utilised in any form or by any electronic, mechanical, or other means, now known or hereafter invented, including photocopying and recording, or in any information storage or retrieval system, without permission in writing from the publishers.

Trademark Notice: Product or corporate names may be trademarks or registered trademarks, and are used only for identification and explanation without intent to infringe.

British Library Cataloguing-in-Publication Data
A catalogue record for this book is available from the British Library

ISBN: 978-1-032-05179-6 (pbk)

Typeset in Chaparral Pro font
Typeset by Aditi Infosystems, Uttar Pradesh, India.

Printed and bound in India.

Table of Contents

List of Figures

List of Tables

Authors' Profile

Sunil Shukla (Ph.D., Psychology)
Director General
Entrepreneurship Development Institute of India
National Team Leader, GEM India
Email: sunilshukla@ediindia.org

Dr. Sunil Shukla, Director General of Entrepreneurship Development Institute of India, Ahmedabad, has been closely working, for more than three decades now, in entrepreneurship education, research, training and institution building. Dr. Shukla has envisioned and designed innovative, outcome based programmes and developmental interventions in the domains of 'entrepreneurship', 'start ups' and 'intrapreneurship' for varied target groups including potential & existing entrepreneurs, innovators, faculty, business executives, bankers, managers, disadvantaged sections, family business successors, administrators and business counsellors. An entrepreneurship exponent, Dr. Shukla's work has also left an indelible impact on the grounds of Greater Mekong Subregion (GMS) countries, Asia, Africa, America, Iran and Uzbekistan. His research work has led to notable policy advocacy and decisions. He leads the largest and the most prestigious annual study of entrepreneurial dynamics in the world – the *Global Entrepreneurship Monitor (GEM) India Chapter*. Today several organizations and departments are benefitting from his guidance and mentorship by having him on their Boards.

Pankaj Bharti (Ph.D. Psychology)
Assistant Professor
Entrepreneurship Development Institute of India
National Team Member, GEM India
Email: pbharti@ediindia.org

Dr. Pankaj Bharti specialises in Organisational Behaviour, Human Resource Management and Corporate Entrepreneurship. He is trained in conceptualising and developing measurement tools for social science research. He holds more than 13 years of experience in academics and industry. He is associated with over 20 National as well as international research projects. He is also a National Team Member of Global Entrepreneurship Monitor (GEM), India and he is co-author of GEM India Report 2014, 2015/16, 2016/17, 2017/18 and 2018/19. His core competency lies in psychometric assessment administration and reporting.

Amit Kumar Dwivedi (Ph.D., Commerce)
Associate Professor
Entrepreneurship Development Institute of India
National Team Member, GEM India
Email: akdwivedi@ediindia.org

Dr. Amit Kumar Dwivedi has over 15 years of teaching and research experience. He has earned a doctoral degree in Industrial Finance from Lucknow University. His areas of interest are Entrepreneurship Education, Family Business and SME Policy. Dr. Dwivedi has published his research in various leading journals. He is part of the India Team that leads the prestigious 'Global Entrepreneurship Monitor' research study. Also, he is co-author of GEM India Report 2014, 2015/16, 2016/17, 2017/18 and 2018/19. Dr. Dwivedi is trained in Application of Simulation for Entrepreneurship Teaching at the University of Tennessee, USA.

Acknowledgements

The GEM India Consortium is glad to probe the conditions that enable entrepreneurship to flourish or deteriorate so that suitable interventions could be accordingly instituted. The consortium has been constantly putting in efforts to research the ways and means that could bolster the entrepreneurship scenario so that the entrepreneurs, the lifeblood of economies, continue to perform a potent role.

The GEM Report 2019–2020 throws light on entrepreneurial trends and practices amidst changing business and economic contours. We express gratitude to the Centre for Research in Entrepreneurship Education and Development (CREED) for providing financial support for this project.

- ❏ Our sincere thanks to the GEM Global Team at London Business School, Babson College and the GEM Data Team for their untiring support and direction.

- ❏ We would also like to heartily thank the national experts and the respondents of various surveys for sparing their valuable time and sharing rich insights with us.

- ❏ We also express our gratitude to Dr. Baishali Mitra, Mr. Zahoor Ahmad Paray, Ms. Hemali Gandhi and Ms. Simran Sodhi, without their support this task could not have been completed.

- ❏ The authors thank Ms. Julie Shah, Head Department of Institutional Communication and Public Relations for facilitating the publication of this report.

- ❏ We express our cordial thanks to the team members of Kantar, India for timely conducting and submitting data of APS.

Authors

Executive Summary

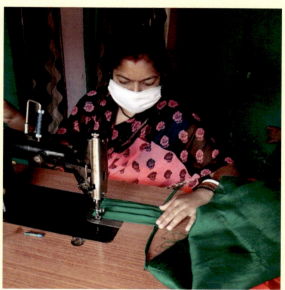

KEY POINTS FROM THE ADULT POPULATION SURVEY (APS)

❏ There is a strong percentage of population who 'know someone who has started a new business'. The data highlights that around 64% of the population knows someone who has started a business recently.

❏ The data shows that 83% of the population perceives that there is a good opportunity to start a business in their area. Of the 50 economies who participated, India has ranked second for perceived opportunities.

❏ The perceived capability has increased as 85% of the population believes they possess skills and knowledge to start a business. The statistics have greatly improved since last year.

❏ As likely as perceived opportunities have increased, the data for fear of failure among youth has also increased. The data shows that fear of failure has increased among people. Fear of failure has increased to 62% of the population to start a business.

❏ A significant change has been observed in entrepreneurship intention in youth. The survey results highlight that entrepreneurship intention has increased from 20.6 % in 2018–19 to 33.3 % in 2019–20.

❏ The data for easy to start business in India for 2019–20 reflects that 80% of the population of the country perceives 'it is easy to start a business in India

❏ The rate of total early-stage entrepreneurship (TEA) in India has also improved and in 2019–20 data TEA in adults has increased to 15% among adults and India now ranks 13th among 50 countries surveyed.

❏ Among female adults TEA has increased significantly as 12% of the total female population is engaged in entrepreneurship in India and 17% of the males are engaged in the same.

❏ The discussion for established business ownership is important. 11.9% of population is engaged in established business.

❏ Another important data to discuss is entrepreneurial employee activity for which India is ranked 47th and only 0.2% of the survey respondents are engaged in it. The data points are zero for females and it is 0.3 for male respondents.

❏ People are majorly motivated by four different reasons to start a business. 86% of the people in India want to start a business to make a difference in the world. The percentage is higher for females and it is 85% males in the population.

❏ Data show that 87% of the population is motivated by 'to build a great wealth' and 83% females and 90% of males from the same.

❏ Among people 79% are motivated because they want to continue their family tradition and it is 81% of females and 78% of males.

❏ People are also motivated to earn a living and it is 87% population who wants to pursue entrepreneurship because of this.

KEY TAKES FROM NES 2019–20

NES survey in India is based on 72 individual experts from field of entrepreneurship, start-up, and academics.

Constraints to entrepreneurship are as under

Among the NES experts, 37% perceive financial support as a major constraint for the strengthening of the entrepreneurship ecosystem of the country.

Experts consider government policy framing and implementation as an important aspect for the development of entrepreneurship in the country.

Experts also consider cultural and social norms, political institutions and social context, and economic climate as important constraints for entrepreneurship growth in the country.

Enablers of entrepreneurship in India are:

The experts highlight government policies their formulation and implementation as important enablers.

Another 26% experts highlight that education and training are vital in enabling entrepreneurship in the country.

Also, 23% experts believe that capacity to entrepreneurs, 16% of experts believe greater financial support and 15% believe access to physical infrastructure are great enablers to entrepreneurship in the country.

RECOMMENDATIONS

The three major points that experts suggest as recommendations are to improve **government policy** and its implementation regarding entrepreneurship development. Introduce and increase **entrepreneurship education** in the country and increase financial support and its reimbursement to the intended entrepreneurs in the country.

1 Business and Entrepreneurship Perspective in India

INDIAN ECONOMY: AN OVERVIEW

Being the fifth-largest economy in the world today, India aims to become the third-largest by 2025. According to historical evidence, India has been a dominant economy with a growing capacity of $5 trillion by 2025. Noting that year 2019 was a difficult year due to slowest economic outcome at 2.9 % globally, since financial crisis of 2009. The impact was also seen on Indian economy as growth in 2019 came down to 4.8 percent from the 6.2 % in 2018–19, amidst a weakening support from global manufacturing trade and demand.

In 2019–20, inflation increased to 4.1% from 3.7% in 2018–19. This increase was mainly recorded due to inflation in food. Historically Indian economy has relied on both invisible hands of the market and a support hand based on ethical and philosophical dimension. For the growth of the economy, it is important to strengthen these invisible hands of the market. This would help in

  i. providing equal opportunities to the new entrants
  ii. eliminating such policies that undermine markets through government intervention
  iii. enabling trade for job creation
  iv. scaling up the banking sector efficiently

In 2019, the government took various actions that contributed towards the upliftment of the market as well as the economy of India. On August 30, 2019 merger of 10 banks was announced, which resulted in the reduction of a number of Public Sector Banks to 12 from 27. This merger helped in better management of banking capital in the country. To become a 5 trillion economy, banks needed to have sufficient money to fund big projects. After the merger, these big banks have competed globally at increased efficiency.

Some initiatives were taken keeping in mind the businesses and startups. These initiatives helped in the smooth and efficient working of businesses. Government of India reduced the Corporate Tax Rate to 22%, which is one of the lowest rates among various countries. Further, to benefit the startups and increase the investments therein, the government announced an exemption from the Angel Tax for startups. Such decisions helped in the growth of businesses and startups which supplemented the growth of the economy. In 2019, RBI also contributed by removing the RTGS and NEFT fund transfer charges. This step was taken to encourage digital transactions in the country. All these steps taken directly and indirectly contributed to the upliftment of the economy. Through such dynamism of government, a better ecosystem was created for the entrepreneurs. A country needs to maintain a healthy ecosystem which lets entrepreneurs grow and also makes it easier for the new entrants to establish themselves in the market.

For strengthening the invisible hands, it is crucial to have a firm entrepreneurial structure in the economy. Strong and growing enterprises not only pump money into the economic structure but also benefit a chain of stakeholders in the market. It is a proven fact, wealth created by an entrepreneur has a strong correlation with benefits to employees. As various enterprises will grow, this would contribute towards the upliftment of many employees, leading towards higher living standards and a healthier economy.

INITIATIVES BY GOVERNMENT TO SUPPORT ENTREPRENEURSHIP, INNOVATION AND STARTUPS

The Government of India takes various initiatives to support entrepreneurs, innovations and startups. Beyond financial backing, the government comes forth with various schemes that are initiated with the target to skill people with the help of workshops. There are other schemes meant to encourage people for startups. Apart from schemes, the government is focusing towards a better ecosystem for entrepreneurs, innovators and startups. Considering this, the government has invested a lot towards infrastructure, incubation centres, innovation centres etc. Following are some of the main highlights of 2019–20 regarding various actions taken by the government:

1. Mahatma Gandhi National Fellowship Programme

With the support of the Ministry of Skill Development and Entrepreneurship (MSDE), Indian Institute of Management, Bangalore launched MGNFP program. This is launched under the SANKALP program of the ministry to skill the youth. The institute welcomed a batch of 75 students on March 08, 2020, with the percentage of 44% women in the batch. This program aims to enhance the skills of the youth. This would further contribute to a better ecosystem for innovations and entrepreneurship.

2. Skills Build Platform

After the UK, Germany and France, India has become the fourth country in the world to launch the Skills Build Platform. This is initiated by the Directorate General of Training under MSDE. The platform aims to train people in information technology, artificial intelligence, networking etc. Training will be provided at ITI (Indian Training Institute) and National Skill Training Institute (NSTI). The program will offer two-year diploma courses in digital technologies.

3. Atal Ranking of Institutions on Innovation Achievements

Atal Ranking of Institutions on Innovation Achievement (ARIIA) is an initiative of the Ministry of Education (MoE). The major aim of this program is to encourage innovation and entrepreneurship at the at the level of educational institutions and universities. This would help in creating a favourable ecosystem at educational platforms for innovations and entrepreneurship. In ARIIA, the Government of India ranks the higher educational institutions and universities based on the innovation and entrepreneurial development of these institutions. This encourages these institutes to have a better ecosystem. The primary indicators for the consideration of ranking include;

❏ budget and funding support
❏ infrastructure and facilities
❏ awareness, promotions and support for idea generation and innovation
❏ promotion and support for entrepreneurship development
❏ innovative learning methods and courses
❏ intellectual-property generation, technology transfer and commercialization
❏ innovation in the governance of the institution

4. Apiary on Wheels

The holistic approach of the Government of India is evident from The Apiary on Wheels Programme. The programme was designed by Khadi and Village Industries Commission. The scheme was launched keeping beekeepers in mind. To support the businesses of beekeepers, the government came up with this idea that helped in the easy and smooth functioning of beekeepers businesses.

There are many other schemes and programs of government which are very progressive and have been functioning since last few years. By the time the Government of India makes few alterations in them according to the necessity, schemes like IMPRINT, Pradhan Mantri Mudra Yojna and Hunar Haat are still considered very helpful by the entrepreneurs and the youth of India. These supports by the government have encouraged many to start their ventures at ample profits.

As per the Economic Survey 2019–20, India has seen a momentous growth at the bottom-of-pyramid entrepreneurship. In recent years, the number of new firms in the formal sector has seen a growth of 12.2%. Further, this year has registered a total of 1,300 startups as well as nine unicorns. These startups alone have created approximately 60,000 direct and 1.3–1.8 lakh indirect jobs.

FIGURE 1.1   Entrepreneurship in India: Key Highlights
Source: States' Startup Ranking, 2019

EASE OF DOING BUSINESS IN INDIA

In Global Innovation Index 2020, India has been ranked at 48 for Ease of Doing Businesses globally. According to the report "Doing Business 2020" by World Bank Group, India is amongst one of those countries which have shown the most notable improvement in doing business. Ease of Doing business focuses on the freedom to do business. Too many government regulations create a burden on entrepreneurs. Under such stringent conditions, entrepreneurs are not able to work freely. This also restricts their creativity and innovativeness sometimes. There are some parameters which decide the parameters of Ease of Doing Business:

  i.   Starting a business
 ii.   Dealing with construction permits
iii.   Getting electricity
 iv.   Registering property
  v.   Getting credit
 vi.   Protecting minority investors
vii.   Paying taxes
viii.   Trading across borders
 ix.   Enforcing contracts
  x.   Resolving insolvency
 xi.   Employing workers

A considerable effort can be observed in the context of trading across borders. Still, India needs to focus more on starting a new business. There are numerous formalities while starting a new business, such as getting permits, property registration etc. This becomes a major hindrance and people avoid entrepreneurship as a career. The ecosystem of India is comfortable for existing businesses, but a bit tedious for the start-ups. To improve its ranking, India needs to be highly focused on ease for startups.

Department of Promotion of Industry and Internal Trade (DPIIT) releases state ranking for Ease of Doing Business in India. DPIIT provides a set of recommendations meant to reduce the time and effort spent by businesses on compliance with a regulation called the Business Reform Action Plan (BRAP). BRAP 2019 is an 80-point list of reforms recommended to simplify, rationalise and digitise the regulatory framework in a state. Andhra Pradesh has been ranked first for Ease of Doing Business in their state in 2019–20. The state has a logistics marvel on the eastern coast. It has a coastline of 974 Km which is the second-longest coastline in India. Andhra Pradesh also has 6 ports, 6 airports, over 1,23,000 km of the road network and 2,600 km of the rail network. This gives the state an advantage of smooth and efficient supply and logistic. Along with this, Sri City Special Economic Zone houses 150 companies from 27 countries, which defines a well-planned infrastructure at a strategic location near Chennai. Another factor which contributes is the Power and Energy efficiency of the state. Andhra Pradesh ranks first in 'Energy Efficiency Implementation Readiness' index of the World Bank. It is the home to the largest single-location solar park.

Nine Unicorns of 2019

FIGURE 1.2 Unicorns registered in India, 2019
Source: *States' Startup Ranking, 2019*

STATES' STARTUP RANKING

The latest buzz is about the ecosystem of the country for entrepreneurs and startups. All the developing, as well as developed economies, are working hard to make their country the most suitable ecosystem for businesses. As per the global ranking, India stands at 23rd position for its startup ecosystem. In 2015, the Government of India announced a flagship initiative 'Startup India' which was designed by the government along with DPIIT. Government came up with the action plan for this initiative in 2016. The very first States' Startup Ranking Exercise under this initiative was conducted in 2018. The major objective of States' Startup Ranking was to encourage all the states and union territories to take the required steps in their respective states/territories that would contribute towards a sound startup ecosystem.

In 2019, the Government of India further developed the framework of the States' Startup Ranking program. For the startup ranking of 2019, few changes were done across seven areas of intervention. These seven pillars of the framework further had 30 action points based on which states' performance would be evaluated.

Participation of 22 states and 3 union territories was witnessed in the Ranking 2019. Out of these states, Gujarat has been given the title for Best Performer followed by Karnataka and Kerala as Top Performer. Among Union Territories, Andaman and Nicobar Islands were ranked as Best Performer. Gujarat has made a considerable attempt across all the pillars. Still, the state requires more attention to Seed Funding.

Because of the States' Startup Ranking, all the states have contributed to make their state the most suitable ecosystem for startups. For the same, every state of India has started online platforms where people can get all the information regarding the aids and support provided by the central and the state governments for startups. It also provides the facility for registration through online mode. Another intervention which was taken seriously by every state was the 'awareness and outreach'. All the states have organised many boot camps for increasing awareness among the people. Many workshops proved to be helpful for the same.

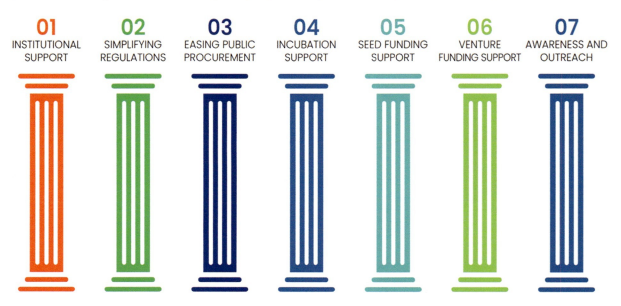

01 INSTITUTIONAL SUPPORT   02 SIMPLIFYING REGULATIONS   03 EASING PUBLIC PROCUREMENT   04 INCUBATION SUPPORT   05 SEED FUNDING SUPPORT   06 VENTURE FUNDING SUPPORT   07 AWARENESS AND OUTREACH

FIGURE 1.3   Basis of intervention in States' Startup ranking
Source: States' Startup Ranking, 2019

The states have framed comprehensive startup policies which help in easy setup and functioning of the businesses. States like Gujarat have a special focus on institutional support, where the states are paying attention to investments in incubation centres. Along with this, states are paying attention towards ecosystem within the educational institutes. Government is funding such institutes that would help the youth of the country to set up their startups with the help of institutional support as well as financial support of the government. All these initiatives across various states combine to form a country with a strong and healthy ecosystem for the startups as well as existing entrepreneurs.

WOMEN ENTREPRENEURSHIP

India is very dedicated to being a self-sufficient country with a suitable ecosystem for businesses and startups. Moreover, GOI is also intensifying on inclusive entrepreneurial boost in the country. This aims to include every section of society and encourage them for entrepreneurial establishment. Talking of inclusivity, women are a very crucial part that needs to be pushed up. For this, GOI comes up with various support systems exclusively for women. In the past decade there has been a significant growth in the number of women entrepreneurs in the country. Studies show that, when women are provided with equal access to resources, the outcomes are equally stronger as that of men entrepreneurs. Not only this but, according to the International

Monetary Fund (IMF), investing in women entrepreneurs can contribute more towards a gradual shift in the society, better education and a healthy environment in the country. Currently, the maximum count of women entrepreneurs has increased in the MSMEs. As per reports, India records 15.7 million women-owned MSMEs and agribusinesses in India. Today women entrepreneurs in India are not limited to small businesses. Breaking the glass ceiling, some women have created some of the most successful startups which are generating annual turnover in crores.

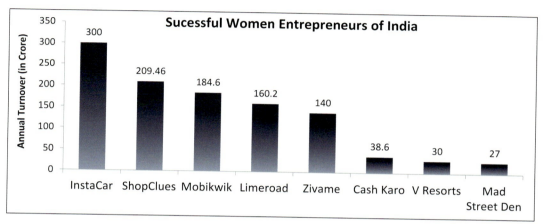

FIGURE 1.4   Successful Women Entrepreneurs in India
Source: Software Success.com

Women entrepreneurs of India contribute 17% in the GDP of the country. However, there is still a lot of scope of improvement in the women's contribution scale in India. Every year the country is converging towards the global average contribution of women entrepreneurs. For completion of this mission, GOI takes several initiatives and organises events to encourage more women to enter the world of entrepreneurship. On January 2019, the National Commission for Women organised an event "Empowering Women through Entrepreneurship" at India Habitat Centre, New Delhi. A similar kind of event was organized with the collaboration of the Ministry of Micro Small and Medium Enterprises in March 2020 at India International Centre, New Delhi. Beyond Central level, the state governments also initiate many such programs to encourage women. In 2019–20 many states like Meghalaya, Sikkim, Tamil Nadu and Jammu and Kashmir organised many events to encourage women for entrepreneurship. Many workshops were conducted to enhance the skills of women in the respective states that would help them to conduct smooth functioning in their business.

2 Global Entrepreneurship Monitor (GEM) Conceptual Framework

Cashew processing unit at Bastar

OVERVIEW

Researchers have invested a long time and efforts to investigate the various nuances of entrepreneurship as a research field. Eventually, several scholarly studies emerged and entrepreneurship is now considered a full-fledged research field and there are numerous research works coming up from different contexts, perspectives, regions and understandings. Many studies have been conducted to understand the complexities of entrepreneurship, its relation to regions, nations, cultures, ecosystem as well as its socio-economic phenomenon. It makes the boundaries of entrepreneurship study highly permeable and the knowledge platform to be fragmented and multidisciplinary. While most of the studies are restricted to a single country or region, they lack uniformity and miss to explain the entrepreneurial qualities of the population. Hence, there have been apprehensions about the understanding of entrepreneurship as a global phenomenon. Consequently, the *GEM Survey* was conceived.

Global Entrepreneurship Monitor (GEM) project, started in 1997 as a collaborative initiative by Michael Hay of London Business School (LBS) and Bill Bygrave of Babson College, USA. The survey was intended for collection and analysis of harmonised data on the prevalence of nascent entrepreneurship and young enterprises across nations. It aimed at generating and propagating knowledge on entrepreneurship globally by exploring the entrepreneurial behaviour and attitude of individuals and the national context, and its effects on entrepreneurship. Since, the first study in 1999, GEM has made substantial contribution to the understanding of entrepreneurship from a global perspective.

GEM global report 2019–20 has provided vibrant details about the participating economies, regions and income levels. The report prefers to call 'economies' instead of countries due to various individual economies that may not be considered as separate economies. There are fifty economies in this latest survey which belong to four different regions and three different economic classifications as defined by the World Economic Forum. There are 11 countries from the Middle East and Africa region whose income varies between low to high. Asia and the pacific region adds eight more economies to the list, ranging from low to high income groups. There are another eight economies from America and the Caribbean region, equally split between middle and high income groups. The largest number of economies is from Europe and North America i.e., 23. Only three out of these 23 are classed as middle-income, while the rest as high-income. Given that the GEM approach is based on people rather than businesses, it helps to capture informal as well as formal economic activity, especially important in low- and middle-income economies. This chapter will also introduce the GEM conceptual framework, the GEM definitions of entrepreneurial activity, and the 50 economies participating in GEM in 2019[1].

TABLE 2.1   Classification of economies participating in the GEM Survey 2019–20

Regions	Low-income	Middle-income	High-income	
Middle East & Africa	Egypt Madagascar Morocco	Iran Jordan South Africa	Israel Oman Qatar Saudi Arabia United Arab Emirates	
Asia & Pacific	India Pakistan	Armenia China	Australia Japan Republic of Korea Taiwan	
Latin America & Caribbean		Brazil Ecuador Guatemala Mexico	Chile Colombia Panama Puerto Rico	

[1]*gem-2019–2020-global-report-rev-280520-1590656414.pdf

Regions	Low-income	Middle-income	High-income
Europe & North America		Belarus North Macedonia Russian Federation	Canada Croatia Cyprus Germany Greece Ireland Italy Latvia Luxembourg Netherlands Norway Poland Portugal Slovak Republic Slovenia Spain Sweden Switzerland United Kingdom United States

Source: GEM Global Report 2019–20

2.1 THE GEM CONCEPTUAL FRAMEWORK

The societal, economic and political contexts to entrepreneurship influence to generate the entrepreneurial environment in a country. The conceptual framework helps to understand the multifaceted phenomenon of entrepreneurship which includes disruptive innovation in products and services, business renewal, job creation, economic expansion, and social wellbeing (GEM global report, 2018). Over the years, the GEM conceptual framework has evolved gradually. This framework and the data analysis help to understand that the entrepreneur is not the only entitlement to economic growth. Instead, it is the environment (ecosystem) which together generates a promising culture of entrepreneurship. An ecosystem of different determinants with individual attributes results in a more sophisticated environment for new ventures and new opportunities to bloom.

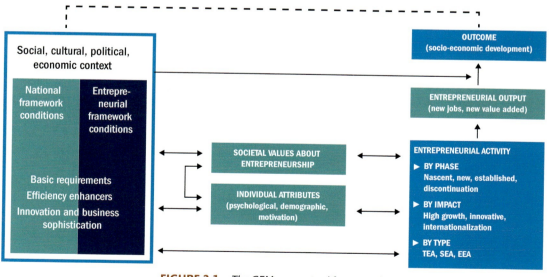

FIGURE 2.1 *The GEM conceptual framework*
Source: GEM Global Report 2018–19

Any country's level of entrepreneurial activity is the result of its population's assessment of entrepreneurial opportunities and their entrepreneurial potential (i.e., motivation and capacity). Recognition of opportunities and entrepreneurial potential are influenced by both specific entrepreneurial framework conditions and general national framework conditions. While entrepreneurial framework conditions are also influenced by the general framework conditions within a nation, both of these are shaped by the social, cultural, political and economic factors. National framework conditions reflect the phases of economic development (factor-driven, efficiency-driven and innovation-driven). The entrepreneurial framework conditions influence entrepreneurial activities directly; these consist of the following factors:

- ❑ **Finance:** The availability of financial resources, equity debt for SMEs (including grants and subsidies) and the extent to which taxes or regulations are either size-neutral or encourage SMEs

- ❑ **Government policies:** The presence and quality of direct programmes to assist new and growing firms at all levels of government (national, regional and municipal)

- ❑ **Entrepreneurial education and training:** The extent to which training in creating or managing SMEs is incorporated within the education and training system at all levels (primary, secondary and post-school)

- ❑ **R&D transfer:** The extent to which national research and development will lead to new commercial opportunities and is available to SMEs

- ❑ **Commercial and legal infrastructure:** The presence of property rights and commercial, accounting, and other legal services and institutions that support or promote SMEs

- ❑ **Entry regulation:** It contains two components: (1) Market dynamics: the level of change in markets from year to year, and (2) Market openness: the extent to which new firms are free to enter the existing markets

- ❑ **Physical infrastructure and services:** Ease of access to physical resources i.e. communication, utilities, transportation, land or space at a price that does not discriminate against SMEs

- ❑ **Cultural and social norms:** The extent to which social and cultural norms encourage or allow actions leading to new business methods or activities that can potentially increase personal income

- ❑ **Senior entrepreneurship:** The availability of policy interventions and social benefits for encouraging senior entrepreneurship

- ❑ **Social values towards entrepreneurship:** It includes how society values entrepreneurship as a right career choice; if entrepreneurs have a high social status; and how media attention to entrepreneurship is contributing (or not) to the development of national entrepreneurial culture.

Individual Attributes

Individual attributes include several demographic factors (gender, age and geography), psychological factors (perceived capabilities, perceived opportunities and fear of failure) and motivational aspects (necessity-based versus opportunity-based venturing, improvement-driven venturing, etc.).

Entrepreneurial Activity

Entrepreneurial activity is defined according to the ventures' lifecycle phases (nascent, new venture, established venture, and discontinuation), the types of activity (high growth, innovation, and internationalisation) and the sector of the activity (Total Early-stage Entrepreneurial Activity or TEA, Social Entrepreneurial Activity or SEA, Employee Entrepreneurial Activity or EEA).

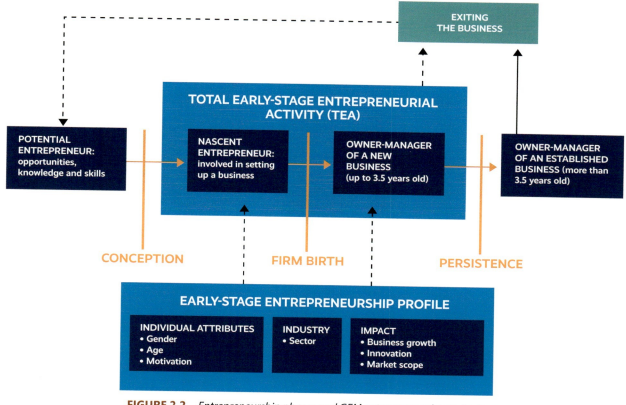

FIGURE 2.2 *Entrepreneurship phases and GEM entrepreneurship indicators*
Source: *GEM Global Report 2019–20*

2.2 GEM OPERATIONAL DEFINITIONS

❏ **TEA:** Percentage of individuals aged 18–64 years who are either a nascent entrepreneur or owner-manager of a new business

❏ **Nascent entrepreneurship rate:** Percentage of individuals aged 18–64 years who are currently a nascent entrepreneur, i.e., actively involved in setting up a business they will own or co-own; this business has not paid salaries, wages or any other payments to the owners for more than three months.

❏ **New business ownership rate:** Percentage of individuals aged 18–64 years who are currently an owner-manager of a new business, i.e., owning and managing a running business that has paid salaries, wages or any other payments to the owners for more than three months but not more than 42 months.

2.3 CHARACTERISTICS OF EARLY-STAGE ENTREPRENEURIAL ACTIVITY

❏ **Opportunity-based early-stage entrepreneurial activity:** The percentage of individuals involved in early-stage entrepreneurial activity (as defined above), who claim to be purely or partly driven by opportunity as opposed to finding no other option for work, includes taking advantage of a business opportunity or having a job but seeking a better opportunity.

❏ **Necessity-based early-stage entrepreneurial activity:** The percentage of individuals involved in early-stage entrepreneurial activity (as defined above), who claim to be driven by necessity (having no better choice for work) as opposed to opportunity

❏ **Improvement-driven opportunity early-stage entrepreneurial activity:** The percentage of individuals involved in early-stage entrepreneurial activity (as defined above), who (1) claim to be driven by opportunity as opposed to finding no other option for work; and (2) who indicate that the main driver for being involved in this opportunity is being independent or increasing their income rather than just maintaining their income.

❏ **High-growth expectation early-stage entrepreneurial activity (relative prevalence):** The percentage of early-stage entrepreneurs (as defined above) who expect to employ at least 20 people five years from now

❏ **New product-market-oriented early-stage entrepreneurial activity (relative prevalence):** The percentage of early-stage entrepreneurs (as defined above) who report that their product or service is new to at least some customers and not many businesses offer the same product or service

❏ **International-oriented early-stage entrepreneurial activity (relative prevalence):** The percentage of early-stage entrepreneurs (as defined above) who report that at least 25 per cent of their customers are from foreign countries

❏ **Established business ownership rate:** The percentage of individuals aged 18–64 years who are currently an owner-manager of an established business i.e., owning and managing a running business that has paid salaries, wages, or any other payments to the owners for more than 42 months

❏ **Business discontinuation rate:** The percentage of individuals aged 18–64 years who in the past 12 months have discontinued a business, either by selling, shutting down or otherwise discontinuing an owner/management relationship with the business. It may be noted that it is NOT a measure of business failure rates.

2.4 INDIVIDUAL ATTRIBUTES OF A POTENTIAL ENTREPRENEUR

❏ **Perceived opportunities** Percentage of the 18–64 years old population who see good opportunities to start a firm in the area where they live

❏ **Perceived capabilities** Percentage of the 18–64 years old population who believe they have the required skills and knowledge to start a business

❏ **Entrepreneurial intentions** Percentage of the 18–64 years old population (individuals involved in any stage of entrepreneurial activity excluded) who intend to start a business within three years.

❏ **Fear of failure rate** Percentage of the 18–64 years old population with perceived opportunities who also indicate that fear of failure would prevent them from setting up a business

2.5 THE GEM METHODOLOGY

The GEM methodology is unique due to its concentration on people rather than businesses. It depends more on the quality and characteristics of people it studies than on enterprises for which data is available globally. This is important, because the attitudes, activities and ambitions of people influence the entrepreneurial process in a society. An economy to grow and sustain needs people and entrepreneurs at every stage, that is, some are starting a new business and some have established a business and sustained into maturity. It helps in bringing a unique profile of entrepreneurship in society. The GEM survey in every participant country is held in two different phases of Adult Population Survey (APS) and National Expert Survey (NES).

The purpose of GEM is to find empirical answers to the following questions:

1. Does the level of entrepreneurial activity vary between countries, and if so, to what extent?

2. Does the level of entrepreneurial activity affect a country's rate of economic growth and prosperity?

3. What makes a country entrepreneurial?
4. What kind of policies may enhance the national level of entrepreneurial activity?

2.6 APS IN INDIA

The APS questions a nationally representative sample of more than 2000 adults about their attitude, motivations, ambitions and activities using the standard global GEM questionnaire. Results and surveys are then checked by GEM global and later approved based on quality and cross-check. APS in every country and India specially brings out the relevant information to informal economy, which is very crucial to the developing world. It helps analyse diverse sets of economic activities, enterprises and jobs that are neither regulated nor protected by the state. With unaccounted informal businesses a country may overlook tax and people may not comply with labour laws. As the GEM survey is random and distributed throughout the population, these activities are easy to be captured and monitored as a part of the entrepreneurship evolution.

A stratified random sampling method is used to select cities or villages across the country. Further, a city/village is divided into four to five strata and selection of a certain number of survey starting points within each city/village is ensured. Moreover, with the help of the Kish Grid method, households and adults were identified for the survey. Rather than selecting the respondents directly from the population, a two-stage sampling method is used. Hence, after identification of the household, the eligible age-group was listed in the descending order by age and an eligible respondent is identified by the Next Birthday method. If a selected person was not available at that time of the initial visit, at least three more visits were made before moving to another household. In all, 3398 respondents aged between 18 and 64 years were included in the survey.

TABLE 2.2 Regional distribution of APS

	Frequency	Percentage	Cumulative Percentage
North	1005	29.6	29.6
West	736	21.7	51.2
South	850	25.0	76.3
East	807	23.7	100.0
Total	3398	100.0	

Source: Based on GEM India Survey 2019–20.

Apart from regional representation, an effort was also made to ensure appropriate representation of gender and location wise i.e., male/female and urban/rural, respectively. For this purpose, appropriate weight was decided on the basis of various criteria.

TABLE 2.3 Rural/urban distribution

Location	Frequency	Percentage	Cumulative Percentage
Urban	2258	66.5	66.5
Rural	1140	33.5	100.0
Total	3398	100.0	

Source: Based on GEM India Survey 2019–20

TABLE 2.4 Gender distribution

Gender	Unweighted sample	Percentage	Cumulative Percentage
Male	1760	51.8	51.8
Female	1638	48.2	100.0
Total	3398	100.0	

Source: Based on GEM India Survey 2019–20

2.7 NES IN INDIA

The second source of the GEM data is the NES conducted via phone, email or in-person interviews on the state of entrepreneurship in the country with 72 national experts from public and private sectors. The interview was conducted with the help of a standardised questionnaire provided under the global GEM project. The local experts were selected for their expertise based on the 'entrepreneurial framework conditions'. They are equipped with rich perspectives not only about their respective profession but also entrepreneurship. The experts are asked to estimate the degree to which each factor of entrepreneurship ecosystem is applicable to India. The final section solicits open-ended responses which are coded to nine categories.

In all, 72 national experts were identified, approached and requested for data provision. Data was collected using e-mails and speed post, followed by face-to-face as well as telephonic interviews. The average work experience of experts was eight years and ranged between 2–27 years.

TABLE 2.5   Working Experience

Mean Experience	8.00
SD	5.85
Range	2–27 Yrs

Expert specialisation includes experts from entrepreneurs, investors, finance specialists, policy makers, business and support service providers. Also included are experts from teaching field and entrepreneurship researchers. The number of participants between these fields differ and education levels also vary.

TABLE 2.6   Experts' Specialisation

S. No.	Specialisation	No.	Percentage
1	Entrepreneur	21	29.2
2	Investor, Financer, Banker	10	13.9
3	Policy Maker	3	4.2
4	Business and Support Services Provider	20	27.8
5	Educator, Teacher, Entrepreneurship Researcher	31	43.1

Source: *Based on GEM India Survey 2019–20.*

The experts as reflected in the below table include people having qualification up to PhD. Some are vocational professionals and university college academicians. The experts also include individuals with PhD and researchers in the entrepreneurship field.

TABLE 2.7   Experts' educational qualification

S.No.	Educational Qualification	Frequency	Percentage
1	Vocational professional	5	6.9
2	University/college	29	40.3
3	MA, Ph.D.	38	52.8
4	Total	72	100.0

Source: *Based on GEM India Survey 2019–20.*

The experts in the NES survey are classified into male and female category as well. In the below table it is clear that there were 11 female and 61 male experts to provide their opinion for the Indian national expert survey.

TABLE 2.7   Expert particulars

Experts	Frequency	Percentage
Female	11	15.3
Male	61	84.7
Total	72	100.0

3 Measuring Entrepreneurship Activity in India

OVERVIEW

This chapter is dedicated to the GEM adult population survey (APS) in India. Adult population survey is a unique data set collected globally, by different GEM teams in more than 50 countries annually. The data is collected every year and more than 2000 adults of each country from various fields relevant to entrepreneurship participate in this country-wide survey. The survey is conducted with adult entrepreneurs, students, nascent entrepreneurs, intended entrepreneurs and others.

Table 3.1 (GEM India snapshot) highlights the significant changes from previous year to the current position of entrepreneurship in India.

TABLE 3.1   *GEM India snapshot*

Attitudes and Perceptions	Value (%)	Rank/50
Perceived opportunity	83.1	2
Perceived capability	85.2	1
Fear of failure	62.4	1
Entrepreneurial intention	33.3	13
Easy-to-start business	80.0	5

Entrepreneurial Activity	Value (%)	Rank
TEA 2019–20	15.0	13/50
TEA 2018–19	11.4	22/48
TEA 2017–18	9.3	31/54
Established business ownership rate	11.9	10/50
Entrepreneurial Employee Activity (EEA)	0.2	47/50

Gender Equity	Value (%)	
Male TEA	17.1	
Female TEA	12.7	
Exited a business in past year	5	
Positive reasons for exit	1.6	
Negative reasons for exit	3.4	

Motivation	% of TEA	Rank/50	% Female TEA	% Male TEA
Make a difference in the world	86.8	1	88.5	85.7
Build great wealth	87.2	3	83.1	90.1
Continue family tradition	36.6	2	81.0	78.9
Earn living because jobs are scarce	64.9	10	84.1	89.9

Source: *GEM Global report 2019–20*

The data analysis in this chapter presents results for perceived opportunities, skills, knowledge of entrepreneurs, motivation, entrepreneurial intentions and entrepreneurial activities in India. A comparison between BRICS countries and the countries in Asia and Pacific is also presented. Regional as well as gender aspect has been discussed in this chapter. The proportion of entrepreneurial activity in India through various means has been included in this chapter. Other data points like total entrepreneurial activity (TEA) in India and its comparison with BRICS, Asia and Pacific countries have also been discussed in the chapter.

TEA data is widespread and includes male-female comparison. TEA across various age groups and in the various regions within India is also included. The chapter also discusses job creation expectations, innovation, and motivations. Industry distribution is another crucial aspect of this attitudinal data. The data further highlights the entrepreneurial motivation and its value among youth and entrepreneurs.

ATTITUDES AND PERCEPTION

As per the GEM definition, respondents' perceptions reflect their intent towards business opportunities for starting a business. These data points in Table 3.2 highlight general notion of the population of the country. The perception of respondents regarding opportunities in their area, perceptions for their perceived capability, the perception for fear of failure and entrepreneurship intentions are given. The data in the table shows that 64% of the population in India perceive that they know someone who has recently started a new business. This data is to understand the impact of new businesses upon the population and also to highlight their possibility of becoming an entrepreneur. The data for opportunities available in their area of interest highlights that more than 83% of adults believe opportunities are available in their area. This also reflects the positive intentions of adults towards entrepreneurship.

Among the surveyed individuals, 80% perceive that it is easy to start a business in India. The statement that whether it is easy to start a business is also an indication of the interest of the population of the country. Perceived intentions lead to actions in the coming time. This percentage has increased mainly due to greater efforts by the government and new policy formulations.

TABLE 3.2 Attitudes and perceptions to start a business in India

Attitudes and Perceptions	Value %	GEM Rank/50
Know someone who has started a new business	64.4	10
Good opportunities to start a business in my area	83.1	2
It is easy to start a business	80.0	5
Personally have the skills and knowledge	85.2	1
Fear of failure (opportunity)	62.4	1
Entrepreneurial intentions	33.3	13

Source: GEM India Survey 2019–20

The individual perceptions for perceived capabilities (personally have the skills and knowledge) increased at a high rate. In this 2019–20 survey, results show that more than 85 of the respondents believed that they personally possess capability to be entrepreneurs. Possessing skills is also considered a determinant of intended entrepreneurs.

The data in the table also highlights that fear of failure among youth has increased as well. Fear of failure has increased from 52.2 (2018) to 62.4 (2019). This is also important to discuss that on one hand, people's perceptions for opportunities have increased, while as their fear of failure has also grown. Fear of failure is very relevant to the middle and lower-income class of society. As entrepreneurship is a task of risk and uncertainty, this statement helps us understand this particular trait among Indians. Fear of failure is inflicted in individuals either naturally or due to social perceptions regarding business.

The data received for intention to start a business has improved from last year. The entrepreneurship intention, as highlighted in 2019 data has increased to 33.3% from previous year results of 2018–19 at 20%. The entrepreneurship intentions for new business creation have improved in ranking as well with new 13th rank among the 50 surveyed economies. Researchers perceive that existence of a good opportunity and having required skills to act upon that, do not necessarily lead to start-up intentions. An idea or an opportunity may trigger in anybody's mind who can think, but ideation and having start-up intentions is a different part of it.

Male Female Attitudes and Perceptions

Male-female comparison of data has been depicted in Fig. 3.1. The data clear that female respondents are more optimistic and perceiving than men. As per the data points, it is easy to start a business is highly perceived by male and female. However, 80% of the females perceive it is easy to start a business and 78% of men perceive that starting a business is easy in India.

Another important aspect is fear of failure which is a common thing and data also proves it. The data for males and females shows similar percentage of fear of failure to start. 56% males and 55% females would not start a business because they fear a failure in business. It happens majorly due to family background and low support to failures. Change of attitudes is important as best entrepreneurs are an outcome of failures. Both males and females depict the intention in other statement but do not want to start business only because they fear they will fail in the business they start.

Another important data point is the knowledge and experience required to start a new business among males and females. The data shows that 81% of males perceive they possess the required skills to start a new business and 85% of the women perceive they possess knowledge and skill to start a business in India. The variation highlights the role of perceptions in human intentions.

Males and females perceive differently about opportunities felt in local area. The data depicts that 80% males perceive they see good opportunity for entrepreneurship and 83% of females perceive they see good opportunities in their local area for new businesses.

There is a variation between male and female respondents for people they know who started a new business. The data depicts that 56% of male members of survey know someone who started a new business and 64% of women believe, they know someone who recently started a business.

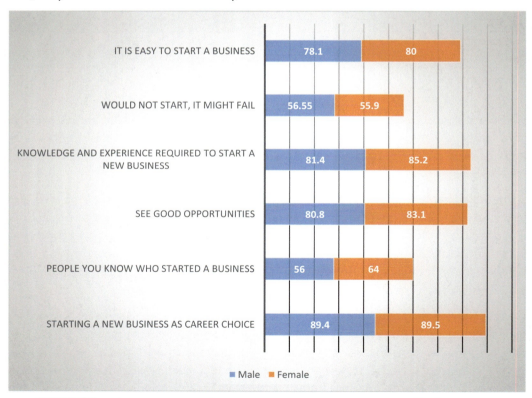

FIGURE 3.1   *Attitudes and perception of males and females: A comparison of BRICS economies*
Source: *GEM India 2019–20*

In Fig. 3.1 the final data points for starting a new business as a career choice reflects that both males and females are on the same page. 89% of male as well as female members quantify that they intend to start a business as a career choice. These are very strong outcomes of the survey and highlight that on the country level things are getting better as this much of percentage is very high and reflects that practical changes are happening and boosting confidence among adults in the country.

ATTITUDES AND PERCEPTIONS TO START A BUSINESS IN BRICS ECONOMIES

Figure 3.2 highlights a comparison of attitudes and perception of respondents for entrepreneurship in BRICS economies. Indians perceive the high level of opportunities and simultaneously possess high fear of failure as well. Indians also show high perception level while answering that they have required skills to start a business. Comparing the data, it is clear that India leads among the BRICS economies for attitudes among adults for available opportunities, skill acquired and fear of failure as well.

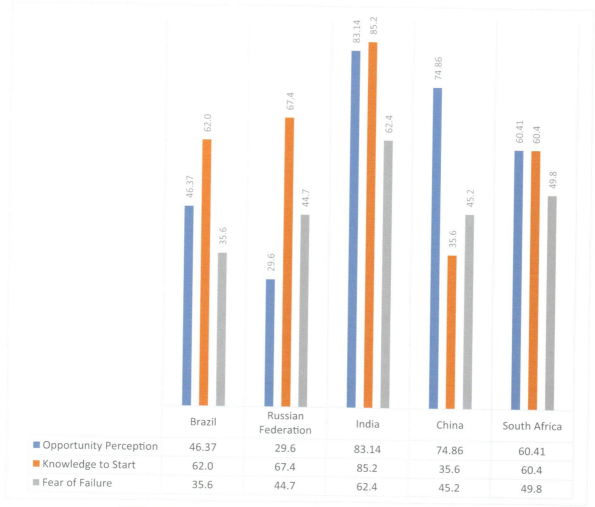

	Brazil	Russian Federation	India	China	South Africa
Opportunity Perception	46.37	29.6	83.14	74.86	60.41
Knowledge to Start	62.0	67.4	85.2	35.6	60.4
Fear of Failure	35.6	44.7	62.4	45.2	49.8

FIGURE 3.2   *Attitudes and perception: A comparison of BRICS economies*
Source: *GEM Global Report 2019–20*

Among BRICS economies lowest perception are affirmed by Chinese respondents, they have low perception for knowledge to start a business in future. Indians perceived highly that they possess knowledge and is followed by respondents in Russian Federation and Brazil.

Another important part of these self-perceptions is fear of failure among people to start a business. The data in Fig. 3.2 shows that while Indians have highly perceived available opportunities, they also perceive high fear of failure. The data shows that 62% of the respondents feared starting a business. The fear of starting a business was highest among BRICS nations followed by respondents from South Africa and then by Chinese respondents of which 45% respondents felt the fear of failure for starting a business.

These perceptions are highly dynamic and keep changing with the government policies and programs. Adults in a country are important to economic activity, while it is clear from research that financial insecurity is the biggest perceived barrier for MSME growth in East Asia and Pacific regions. There may be other reasons but improvement in perception for opportunities does not mean an improvement in the fear of failure.

SELF-PERCEPTION TO START A BUSINESS IN EAST ASIA AND PACIFIC COUNTRIES

Figure 3.3 highlights a comparison of differences of perceptions between economies throughout South Asia and Pacific regions of the world. The data compare Armenia, China, Australia, Japan, Pakistan, Republic of Korea and Taiwan. The comparison is important due to its economic, regional and perceptional relevance. The data comparison highlights that for perception of available opportunities, India leads, followed by China, and Pakistan where 62% of the respondents show a high perception towards available opportunities.

Looking into the Fig. 3.3, it is clear that high percentage of respondents are positive regarding the knowledge to start a business in their country. India leads with 85% of the population perceiving that they possess knowledge to start a business in their country. The country is followed by Armenia where 70% of respondents believe they possess enough knowledge to start a business. Armenia is followed by China and China is followed by Pakistan at 63% of respondents perceiving high knowledge to start a business.

As likely Indians perceive great opportunities and knowledge. Indians are also full of fear of failure as depicted in Fig. 3.3. The data also reveals that more than 62% of Indians believe they have a fear of failure to start a business in the country. The fear of failure is lowest among the people of Republic of Korea. Only 7% Koreans perceive fear of failure and it is an important statistic to analyse here. Smaller economies are more confident and perceive low fear of failure for business creation. More than 40% of the Koreans believe they find an opportunity in their country and 40% of Koreans also believe they have a skill to start a business in their country. In both the analyses India has firmly positioned itself and has been continuously increasing and improving its business environment and possible business growth.

Region-wise Perceptions and Attitudes

The GEM survey includes samples from every region of the country. Among the four regions of India, opportunities are highly perceived in Northern respondents followed by those in the West, East and South. A total of 87% population in north India perceives opportunity to start a business. Figure 3.4 also confirms that perceived capability is also highly observed by people in the north India followed by west India.

The data highlight the regional variation for perceived opportunities and perceived capabilities in the country. The data also identifies that it is easier to start a business in western region of India and duly followed by northern region of the country. South India is consistently low in these statistics and clearly highlights a need for more intervention. This also makes it clear that regional difference is visible in the Fig. 3.4.

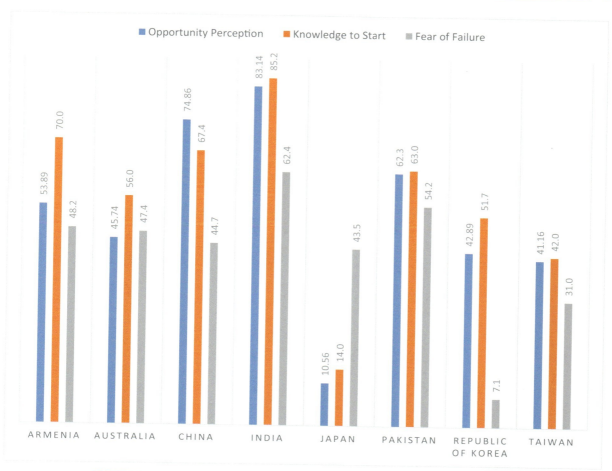

FIGURE 3.3 *Attitudes and perception: A comparison of East Asia and Pacific countries*
Source: *GEM Global Report 2019–20*

ENTREPRENEURIAL ACTIVITY IN INDIA

Total entrepreneurial activity is the total percentage of the population involved in new business or existing business in the country. In this section, majorly the TEA, business ownership, and entrepreneurial employee activity are discussed. Data also identifies important nuances for economies where demographic dividend is evident and a clear impact is seen. In India, every year data is collected to identify entrepreneurship activity among various age groups.

TEA in India

In Table 3.3 total early stage entrepreneurial activity identifies that 15% of the adults in the country are involved in some way into business doing either a new or nascent business. India is ranked 13th in the total TEA rankings among 50 countries. As per TEA in India 12.7% females and 17% of males are involved.

The data in the Table 3.3 also highlights established business ownership rates and it is relatively high with 11% of the total adults in the country involved in established businesses and with a ranking of 10 in the GEM survey. The difference between males and females is evident here too, as only 9% females are involved in established business and more than 14% males are involved in the established businesses in the country.

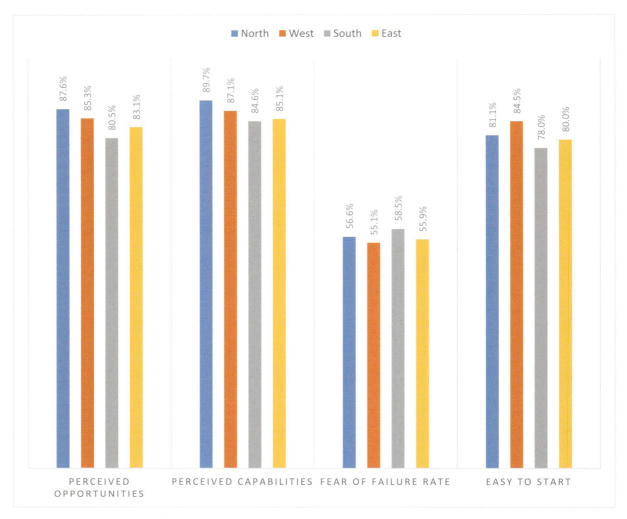

FIGURE 3.4   *Perception and Attitudes: A comparison of Indian region*
Source: GEM India Survey 2019–20

Entrepreneurial employee activity is also an important perspective in this analysis. Data identifies that only 0.2% adults in the country perceive that they are contributing to entrepreneurial activity in the country. India ranks 47th in this and zero percentage of females contribute to it and only 0.3% males perceive any type of entrepreneurial employee activity.

TABLE 3.3   *TEA, EBA and EEA in India*

	% Adults	Rank/50	% Female	% Male
Total early-stage Entrepreneurial Activity	15.0	13	12.7	17.1
Established business ownership rate	11.9	10	9.1	14.6
Entrepreneurial Employee Activity	0.2	47T	0.0	0.3

Source: GEM India Survey

Region-wise TEA in India

It is evident in the data (Fig. 3.5) that TEA varies within Indian regions. The recent reports of 2017–18 and 2018–19 also identified this difference in variations. The differences are majorly caused by the difference of the economic status of the states as well as the entrepreneurial culture in the country. The entrepreneurship is praised in certain regions and certain regions meagerly prioritize it. The typical reason for lower TEA in one region and higher in other may be explained by the fact that western region of the country is more entrepreneurial, more business exist there, industries and work environment is suitable while other regions are half mountainous, or poorer than other regions. There may be many causes to the less involvement of regions in entrepreneurial activity but, entrepreneurship is growing in the country and is flourishing in the facts discussed in the GEM India snapshots.

The data highlights that respondents in the northern region of the country have a higher percentage of population involved in total entrepreneurial activity. Followed by south India where a total 16% people are involved in TEA. In this 2019–20 survey, it is also clear that only 13% of respondents from western region are involved in the total entrepreneurial activity. The proportion of TEA highlighted in this 2019–20 data is surprising to some extent as recent GEM India studies identified different regions as high TEA. This identifies a changing dynamic of entrepreneurship in the country where regional aspirations are changing and new businesses are emerging throughout.

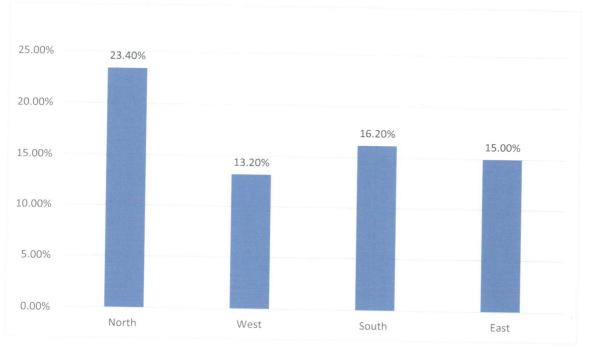

FIGURE 3.5   *Region-wise TEA in India (% of the adult population aged 18–64 years)*
Source: *GEM India Survey*

TEA Comparison of Last Three Years Age Groups

In Fig. 3.6 data for a comparison of TEA for three consecutive years is given. Latest data for TEA in India highlights good improvement over the preceding years. The improvement is visible in the latest year of data collection 2019–20. The data shows that 14% of the adults in the age group of 18–24 are involved in TEA and more than 16% of the population is active in TEA in the age group of 25–34. The data is also depictive of the picture that TEA among age groups 35–44 and 55–64 has greatly gained ground. The only age group which has not improved comparing to last year is in 45–54 age group. The results for the survey conducted in 2019–20 have shown a constant rise in TEA for all age groups.

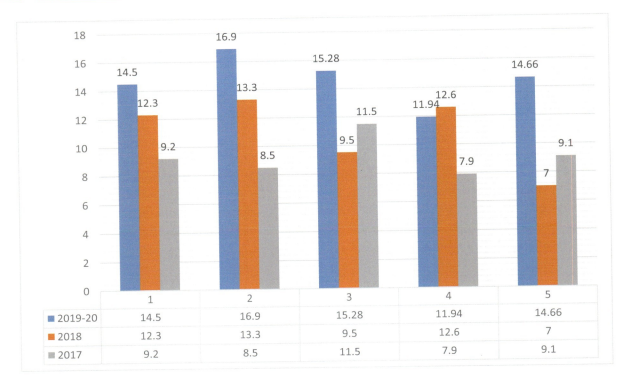

	1	2	3	4	5
■ 2019-20	14.5	16.9	15.28	11.94	14.66
■ 2018	12.3	13.3	9.5	12.6	7
■ 2017	9.2	8.5	11.5	7.9	9.1

FIGURE 3.6   *TEA by age groups in India comparison of last three years*
Source: *GEM Global Report 2019–20*

Gender-wise TEA in BRICS Economies

Total entrepreneurial activity is a significant indicator in this GEM data collected globally. There are various outcomes. Figure 3.7 shows how BRICS countries perceive TEA in their respective countries. The results in the figure depict a high percentage of 23% male and 23% of female respondent's involved in entrepreneurial activity. The data also highlights that in India 12% of females and 17% of males are engaged in entrepreneurship. The graph also shows that in Russia a little difference of percentage can be seen. Only 8% of the women and 10% of the males are engaged in entrepreneurial activity in Russian federation in 2019–20. The lowest of TEA is depicted by people in China, only 7% of females and 9% of males are engaged in entrepreneurial activity. The results are clearly depictive of the gender gaps and entrepreneurial capability in these countries. The results also verify a significant need for the improvement of gender inequalities in these societies which seems low in Brazil, India and China.

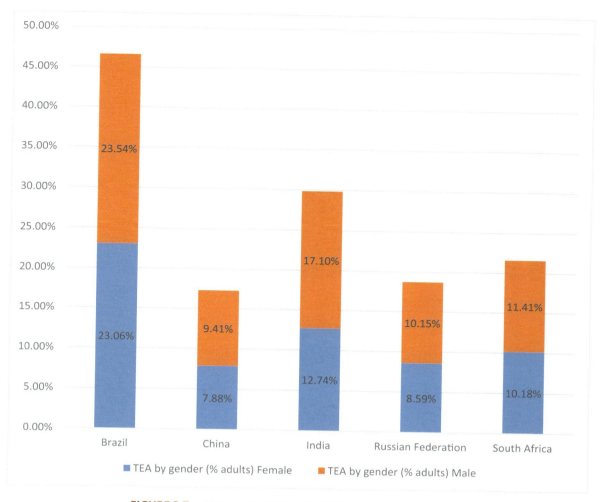

FIGURE 3.7   *TEA in male and female: A BRICS economies comparison*
Source: *GEM Global Report 2019–20*

Age Groups and TEA among BRICS Economies

Figure 3.8 provides a comparison of the entrepreneurship at various age groups among BRICS economies. The most ideal age to begin entrepreneurship is in the age group 18–24. The data is predictive of high entrepreneurship in Brazil in this age group. It shows that 24% of the people are engaged in entrepreneurship in the age group of 18–24. People in process of either starting a new business or those who already have one, are in the age group of 18 and 64 years and are considered as a part of the total entrepreneurial activity (TEA) in a country. India follows as the second highest with 14% people engaged in entrepreneurship in the age group of 18–24.

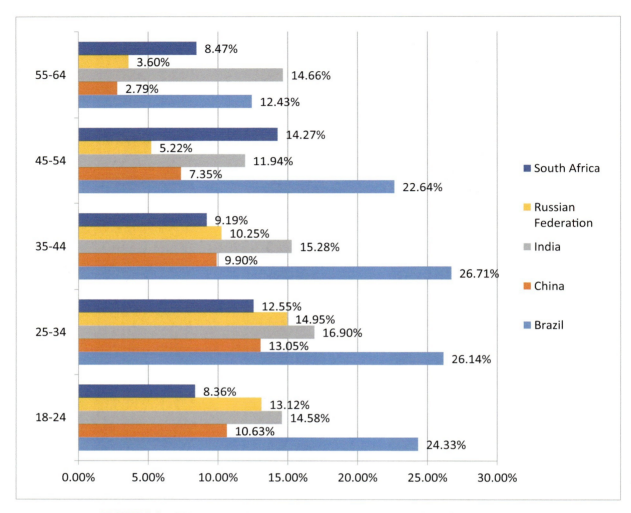

FIGURE 3.8   *TEA in various BRICS economies: A comparison (% of population aged 18–64)*
Source: *GEM Global Report 2019–20*

The second age group 25–34, considered more mature and relevant for the entrepreneurship endeavors are highest in Brazil with 26 and India with 16% respondents in this age group engaged in TEA. Another age group in this survey is 35–44 and in this age group Brazil leads among BRICS nations and it is shown that 26% of the respondents belong to this entrepreneur's age group. It is again followed by India and Russian federation afterwards.

In the age group of 45–54, Brazil leads among BRICS economies and in the age group of 55–64 India leads with a 14% people starting a business at this age. The percentage is high in Brazil with 12% people doing a business activity in that country. Respondents of China are continuously low in these statistics and clarify that TEA among varied age groups is low. Here it is important to note that entrepreneurship is low and high in different countries. This confirms that old people possess more sources and networks to start business in comparison to young aged (18–24) in some countries. This gives an important detail of the total entrepreneurial activity in India and also clears that TEA is high in the age group of 25–34 and is expected to rise. It is important to mention here that the entrepreneurship measurement mentioned above includes organizational lifecycle approach i.e., nascent, new business, established business or nascent entrepreneurs.

OPPORTUNISM, PROACTIVITY, INNOVATIVE CAPACITY AND VISION

Perceptions, proactivity, innovativeness and vision identify the future youth in business. Opportunism is the realization that youth rarely see any opportunity to do business. Proactivity is the possibility of acting on an opportunity sighted by the youth. Innovative capacity is the percentage of the population who agree other people think they are innovative. Also, vision clears that every decision of the youth is a part of their long-term career plan. This data is significant for the countries like India which envisions a growth of start-ups in the coming years and expects a huge surge of start-ups and businesses for the employment growth and economic upliftment of the population.

The data in Fig. 3.9 shows that 77% of the Indian respondents perceive a vision and 70% of them perceive they are innovative. It is also observed that 66% of Indians perceive they are proactive and 71% of the respondents perceive being opportunistic. India leads among BRICS economies for these data points and clears that entrepreneurship and its features are growing in the country. These data points are recently modified in the GEM methodology to give a clear vision of the youth of these economies.

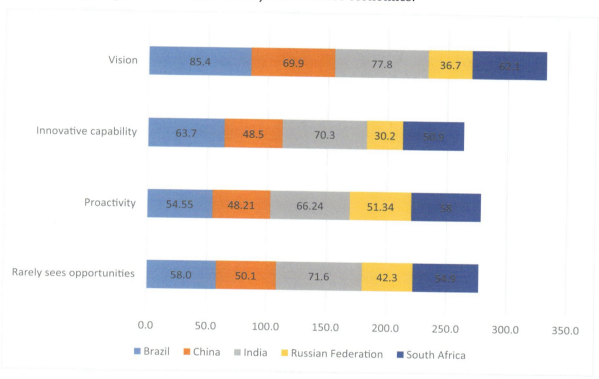

FIGURE 3.9   *A comparison of BRICS countries*
Source: *GEM Global Report 2019–20*

Nascent, New Business and Established Business Ownership Rate

Nascent business ownership, new business ownership and established business ownership rates are three different indicators of entrepreneurship progress in India and other economies. Nascent are those individuals in the age group 18–65 who are in the process of starting a business but nothing concrete has emerged. In Fig. 3.10 data highlights that 9.4% of the Indians own a nascent business. Comparing data with other emerging countries in the world we find that among these countries highest number of Indians own nascent enterprises.

New business ownership rate shows businesses that have started but did not pay any salary to employees. The new enterprise ownership rate in India is 5.9 but the highest is in Brazil where 15 people possess a new business. This gives rise to many new generalizations and perspectives of new business creation in different countries. Other countries which show high new business ownership rate are Russian Federation (4.8), China (3.6) and Japan (2.1). This is an important factor to understand the current position of entrepreneurship in a country.

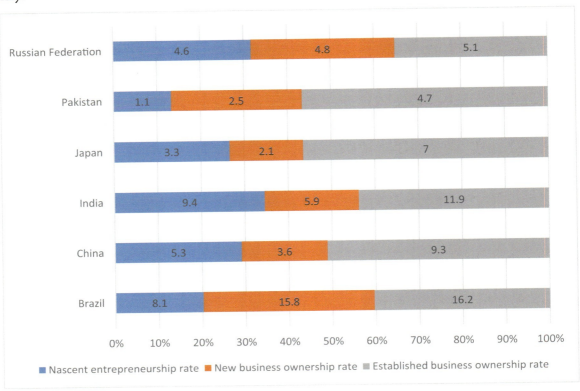

FIGURE 3.10 *Nascent, New Business and Established Business Ownership Rate economies*
Source: *GEM Global Report 2019–20*

The established business rate highlights businesses established sometime back and have paid their first salaries to the employees. Information regarding the level of established businesses in a country is essential as it indicates the sustainability of entrepreneurship in a country. Most of these businesses have passed the start-up and new business stage. These enterprises are ready to contribute to the country's employment and growth by introducing new products and processes. The data highlights that established business ownership rate is highest in Brazil (16) followed by India at 11.9% and China (9.3). Other countries which follow in this indicator are Russian Federation, Japan and Pakistan.

Business Exit and Discontinuation

The business exit and discontinuation are both different entities, varying in different economies. Economic condition, personal, and finance are major reasons for discontinuation and exits. People exit either to join or start a venture or to discontinue a business. On the other hand, discontinuation may happen due to lack of business profitability, problems with accessing finance and running out of working capital. Business exit rate is evident and highest in China followed by Brazil, India and South Africa. Another important data point in Fig. 3.11 is how many people exited a business but business continued. The statistics show that China has the highest exit and continue rates followed by India with 2.1% people exiting a business but businesses continue.

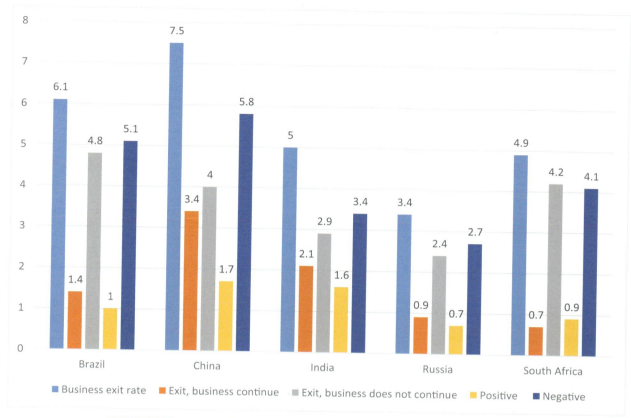

FIGURE 3.11   *Business Exit and Discontinuation: A comparison of selected economies*
Source: GEM Global Report 2019–20

The business in the 2019–20 also discontinued due to exit of the people. Figure 3.11 highlights that with 4.8% of the population exited a business which was later on discontinued. The rate is high in South Africa as well and as in China with 4% of the population exiting a business which then discontinued. The data points for India show that 2.9% people exited a business and business got discontinued.

The data also highlights the reason for exit and in Fig. 3.11, it can be seen that least of the respondents gave a positive reason for business exit. As evident in the graph, only 1% of the people exited a business due to positive reasons and 5.1% exited due to negative reasons in Brazil. This was followed by China with only 1.7% people exiting due to positive reasons and 5.8% exited due to negative reasons. In India 1.6% exited due to positive reasons and 3.4% due to negative reasons which then discontinued the business.

MOTIVATION FOR ENTREPRENEURSHIP

Individual motivation is a primary source of new businesses. In this latest 2019–20 data survey, questions for motivation are more clearly drafted and seek answers for what motivates people for entrepreneurship throughout the world. In India motivations for business are majorly due to job scarcity, opportunities, growing market and family reasons. Motivation for entrepreneurial activity depends upon the resource access of an individual (Aldrich & Zimmer, 1986). The source of motivation varied throughout the economies which participated for GEM 2019–20.

Table 3.4 provides data for both males, females and percentage of TEA. The data reveals that globally entrepreneurs want to make a difference in the world. It is highest in India, 86% of the total TEA want to make a difference in the world and is followed by South Africa where 85% of the entrepreneurs want to make a difference in the world. The data are high in both the gender categories as well. In India and South Africa 85% males, 88% females and 82% male and 87% females, respectively, are committed to make a difference in the world. From this data, it is clear that female percentage is higher for their motivation to make a change in the world.

Another important perspective in this series of outcomes is whether entrepreneurs build to make a great wealth or high income out of their business. The data reveals that the highest percentage (88%) of Indian adults seek entrepreneurship to build a great wealth and increase income. India is followed by South Africa with 78% of the population and 69% of the Russian Federation population consider wealth creation as a major objective behind their entrepreneurial journey. Males are more inclined as percentages show that percentage of males is higher than females who want to increase wealth and generate high income out of their businesses.

TABLE 3.4   *Entrepreneurial Motivation: A comparison of East Asia and Pacific*

Motivation to start a business	To make a difference in the world			To build great wealth or very high income		
Country name	% of TEA	% of Male TEA	% of Female TEA	% of TEA	% of Male TEA	% of Female TEA
Brazil	51.4	49.6	53.2	36.9	41.9	31.8
China	39.7	36.7	43.9	48.4	54.0	40.8
India	86.8	85.7	88.5	87.2	90.1	83.1
Russian Federation	27.1	25.6	28.7	69.7	70.8	68.5
South Africa	85.0	82.9	87.1	78.9	83.6	74.0
Average	58.0	56.1	60.3	64.2	68.1	59.6

Source: GEM Global Report 2019–20

More than 70% of the businesses in the world are dominated by families and doing business is a family affair. The question is whether entrepreneurs are motivated to continue family tradition. The percentage is highest in India again as there is a huge percentage of businesses in India run by families. Family has a great role to play in career choices of many budding entrepreneurs. It is also high in South Africa and China. A higher percentage of male TEA is motivated to do business and continue the family tradition.

The jobs are a scarce affair in many of the prominent countries and India is also facing the same with many other. Scarcity of jobs or necessity to earn sometimes motivates people to become entrepreneurs. The percentage of TEA who were motivated because jobs are scarce in their country is evident in Table 3.5. The data highlights that in South Africa 90% of the entrepreneurs are motivated by it and more than 88% in Brazil, 87% in India and 78% in Russian Federation. It shows that the job scarcity is not just related to East Asia but countries outside it are also facing the same problem. Among males it is clear that in India 89% are motivated for entrepreneurship due to the scarcity of jobs in the country and the same percentage of adults in South Africa are motivated to be entrepreneurs. It is more than 91% in South Africa, 90% in Brazil and 84% in India that females are motivated for entrepreneurship in these countries.

TABLE 3.5   *Entrepreneurial Motivation: A comparison of East Asia and Pacific*

Motivation to Start a Business	To continue a family tradition			To earn a living because jobs are scarce		
Country name	% of TEA	% of Male TEA	% of Female TEA	% of TEA	% of Male TEA	% of Female TEA
Brazil	26.6	28.8	24.4	88.4	86.0	90.8
China	40.6	33.8	50.0	65.8	64.2	68.0
India	79.8	78.9	81.0	87.5	89.9	84.1
Russian Federation	24.9	26.4	23.3	78.8	76.0	81.7
South Africa	48.0	43.7	52.5	90.3	89.4	91.2
Average	44.0	42.3	46.2	82.1	81.1	83.2

Source: GEM Global Report 2019–20

The data results highlight that many things motivate a person to be an entrepreneur and among them going for a family business, making a difference in the world and to earn a living due to scarcity of jobs are critical to these factors.

GROWTH EXPECTATION

Growth is a very diverse phenomenon and is used in diverse ways. It is related to employment growth, innovation growth, sales growth, technological progress and others. These identifications of growth are very important and help us identify the prospects of a certain industry or enterprise. In GEM study, growth expectations are related to the percentage of 18–64 population who expect to increase a particular number of employees in the coming years. In a country like India population is huge and is increasing year on year. The growth of jobs and work must encompass population growth which can lead to economic growth of the country.

The data listed in Table 3.6 is given for entrepreneurship impact in India. The data shows that only 1.6% of the TEA are expecting a growth of more than six new employees in their business. The data highlights the expectations from the near future and clarifies that a small percentage of entrepreneurs perceive employee growth in their businesses.

Another important aspect highlighted in this table is the revenue generated from international business. It is also important to understand the international business potential of India. Only 0.1% adults in India confirm they earned their 25% or more revenue from international business transactions. India is at 49th rank for revenue generated from international business.

The data in Table 3.6 presents important information regarding the scope of customers and products/processes. The data identifies that only 0.3% of TEA verify their products and processes compatible for national scope. India has 45th rank for global scope of their customer's products and processes. The ranking and 0.0 percentage of adults identifies need for interventions to improve ranking and percentage of Indian TEA for global presence.

The country ranks 47th for industry percentage in business services. The data here gives that 3.3% of the TEA perceive that they are in business services. These statistics identify strengths, weaknesses and possibilities for improvement through this entrepreneurship impact data (Table 3.6).

TABLE 3.6 *Entrepreneurial Impact: A comparison of East Asia and Pacific*

Entrepreneurship Impact	% Adults	Rank/50
Job expectations (6+)	1.6	38T
International (25%+ revenue)	0.1	49T
National Scope (customers and products/process)	0.3	42T
Global scope (customers and products/process)	0.0	45T
Industry (% TEA in Business Services)	3.3	47

Source: *GEM Global Report 2019–20*

Employment Growth Expectation

In this section growth of the TEA is discussed. The TEA in a country leads us to understand the entrepreneurial activity and growth explains the plans for employing new people in order to achieve growth. The data highlights that more than 7% of Armenians do not expect any increase in the number of employees in their business. Nearly 7% Indians also believe they will not add any new employee to their business and the same percentage is high in Republic of Korea and China.

There is a significant percentage of TEA that considers increasing 1–5 employees in their business in next five years. The data is clear that around 7% of Armenians and 3.2% of Republic of Korea expect to increase employment. However, the percentage in India is 6.4 which means a significant number of business are planning to engage 1–5 new employees in their business.

Around 6% of the TEA in Armenia want to increase employee strength by six or more in coming years. The percentage is half in Republic of Korea and keeps decreasing with other economies. It is only 1.6% of total TEA in India who want to increase employment and only 0.5% of TEA in Pakistan who want to increase their employment by 6 or more people in the next five years.

TABLE 3.6   *Employment projection for the next five years by TEA in India (% of population aged 18–64 years)*

Economy	Job Creation Expectations		
	0 jobs	1–5 jobs	6 or more jobs
Armenia	7.7	6.9	6.4
Australia	3.6	4.3	2.6
China	5.4	1.6	1.7
India	6.9	6.4	1.6
Japan	2.4	1.5	1.5
Pakistan	1.8	1.4	0.5
Republic of Korea	6.1	5.6	3.2
Taiwan	3.4	2.4	2.5
Average	4.7	3.8	2.5

Source: GEM Global Report 2019–20

The new addition of questions in this section highlights the customer strength of the business in these economies. The data shows that 0.3% of the TEA believe their products are suitable for national markets and the percentage is high in Armenia (2.5), Taiwan (2.5), and 1.3 in Japan.

In this data table (Table 3.7), numbers help us identify which country's TEA has high customers from international markets and products suitable for outside markets. The data reveals that very low percentage of TEA identifies their products and processes suitable for global markets. In India and Pakistan 0.0 percentage of TEA perceive they have not acquired any customers from global or international markets. At the end of the data table, TEA percentage perceive that 25% of their revenue will originate from outside the country. The data shows that 4% of the Armenian TEA expect their 25% revenue from outside the country. While as only 0.4% form China, 0.1% form India and 0.2% from Pakistan believe their revenues will emerge from outside their country.

TABLE 3.7   *Employment projection for the next five years by TEA in India (% of population aged 18–64 years)*

Economy	At least national scope for its customers and new products or processes	Global scope for its customers and new products or processes	Expecting 25% or more of revenue from customers outside own economy
Armenia	2.5	0.4	4.0
Australia	1.7	0.5	1.3
China	0.3	0.1	0.4
India	0.3	0.0	0.1
Japan	1.3	0.2	0.5
Pakistan	0.2	0.0	0.2
Republic of Korea	1.8	0.3	0.5
Taiwan	2.5	0.6	0.7
Average	1.3	0.3	1.0

Source: GEM Global Report 2019–20

INDUSTRY SECTOR PARTICIPATION IN INDIA

Industry sector participation in this survey represents various types of businesses which participate in the survey. The results collectively provide data about the concentration of businesses in different sectors. In the year 2019–20, various sector businesses participated including agriculture, mining, finance, professional services, administrative services, personal consumer services and wholesale and retail. Figure 3.12 shows data for Indian business sector concentration. The data highlights that 61% of the total TEA in India is engaged in wholesale and retail businesses. Another high concentration is from manufacturing sector (11.9) followed by health, education, government and social service sector. The data also provides information for other important sectors in India such as agriculture, mining, transportation, professional services and others in which Indian TEA participates.

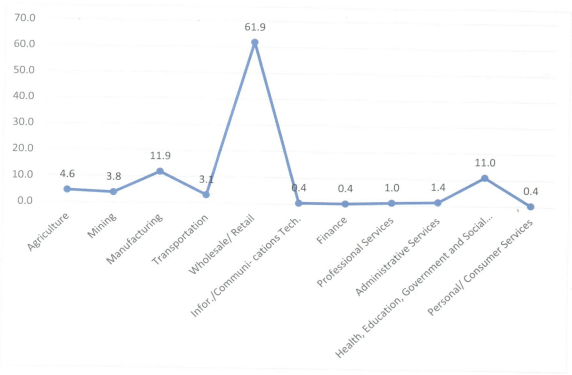

FIGURE 3.12   *Distribution of sectors in India*
Source: *GEM India survey*

Sector-wise Distribution of Industries in BRICS Economies

The global entrepreneurship survey conducted in different economies identifies retail and wholesale as the two most important forms of businesses being run in every economy. The data in Fig. 3.13 highlights that majority of the respondents in BRICS economies are also in the same type of business and industry and it is followed with variation by enterprises in health, education, government and social sector. The data is also clear that highest number of retail and wholesale businesses as identified in survey are run in India. Besides these people are also involved in other sectors like, professional services, finance, agriculture and mining. Every other sector is marginally being represented in India and other BRICS economies. There is a growing percentage of businesses in manufacturing sector as well. The important sector in the BRICS as identified in the graph are health, education, government and social services, transportation, manufacturing, mining, agriculture. These highlight concentrated percentages among various sectors in Fig. 3.13.

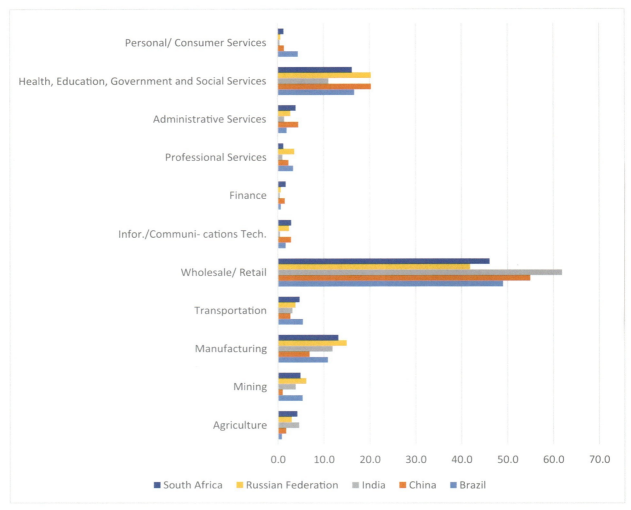

FIGURE 3.13   *Industry sector participation of % of TEA in BRICS Economies*

Source: GEM Global Report 2019–20

APS country survey in India was conducted with more than 4000 people in 2019–20. The data has been analyzed with SPSS to understand the various outcomes of the survey. The data results point that various nuances of entrepreneurship in the country have changed and changed for better. Most of the data points such as perceived opportunity, perceived capability, easy to start a business have improved from 2018–19 survey. This adds to the countries' efforts being made for entrepreneurship development in the country.

4 Entrepreneurship Framework Conditions in India: National Expert Survey (NES)

OVERVIEW

Annually, the Global Entrepreneurship Monitor (GEM) comes up with the entrepreneurial trends and ecosystem around the world. For a holistic understanding it tries to understand the multiple factors that lead to enhance (or hinder) the business creation in the economies. Amongst many, Entrepreneurial Framework Condition (EFC) is one of the most important pillars of the entrepreneurial ecosystem. For the assimilation of EFC, the Global Entrepreneurship Monitor has adopted National Expert Survey as a methodology to assess the conditions and understand the ecosystem in the respective economies. To carry out this research, GEM has networked with the national country teams which are associated primarily with top academic institutions. The unique tools of GEM benefits numerous stakeholders like; academicians, policymakers, entrepreneurs, sponsors and international organizations. The National Expert Survey (NES) provides a uniform and harmonised measure for understanding the framework. For the collection of data, NES uses the questionnaire with is administered to a minimum of 36 experts in each GEM country. The questionnaire allows the measurement of nine key EFCs (Fig. 4.1).

FIGURE 4.1   Entrepreneurial framework conditions
Source: About National Expert Survey, GEM

ENTREPRENEURSHIP FRAMEWORK CONDITIONS: COMPARISON OF LOW-INCOME COUNTRIES

The GEM survey has considered 12 different parameters on the basis of which we can have a comparison between the low-income economies and Indian economy. These 12 parameters are the extension of 9 factors of NES mentioned earlier. Overall, the performance of India is admirable. Across all 12 parameters, India is ahead of the low-income country performances. Out of all, India has contributed tremendously towards entrepreneurship education at school stage. As we observe the stand of low-income economy, we can witness lower figures as compared to India. India is also putting a lot of efforts towards the research and development transfer followed by government policies. Indian government is very supportive towards the policy which contributes in supporting the startups and existing enterprises.

But, still India has to exert more efforts on physical infrastructure. The country has devoted noticeable efforts in physical infrastructure but when compared to low-income countries, India has almost same numbers in the records. Another factor which requires attention is the entrepreneurship education at post-school stage. In this area, the country has not performed very well. On the other hand, entrepreneurship education at school stage has recorded a meritable position. But the condition of entrepreneurship education at post school stage is opposite as well as alarming. (Fig. 4.2)

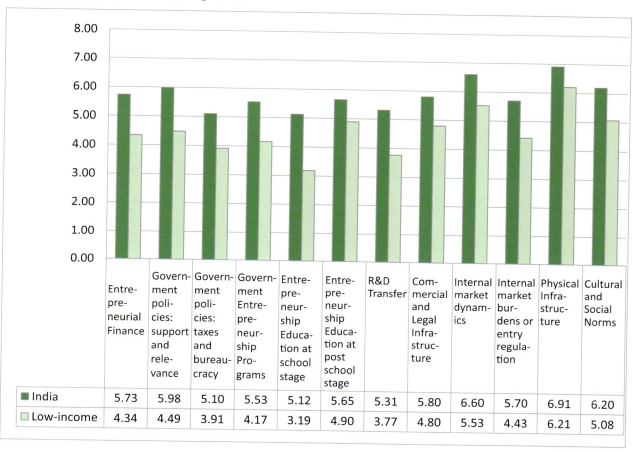

	Entre-pre-neurial Finance	Govern-ment poli-cies: support and rele-vance	Govern-ment poli-cies: taxes and bureau-cracy	Govern-ment Entre-pre-neur-ship Pro-grams	Entre-pre-neur-ship Educa-tion at school stage	Entre-pre-neur-ship Educa-tion at post school stage	R&D Transfer	Com-mercial and Legal Infra-struc-ture	Internal market dynam-ics	Internal market bur-dens or entry regula-tion	Physical Infra-struc-ture	Cultural and Social Norms
India	5.73	5.98	5.10	5.53	5.12	5.65	5.31	5.80	6.60	5.70	6.91	6.20
Low-income	4.34	4.49	3.91	4.17	3.19	4.90	3.77	4.80	5.53	4.43	6.21	5.08

FIGURE 4.2 Comparison of low-income countries and India
Source: GEM India Survey

ENTREPRENEURIAL FRAMEWORK CONDITIONS, BRICS NATIONS

When the performance of India and the BRICS nations is compared, we can observe that India is performing well across all the pillars. In fact, out of all, India is a leading performer in four factors of entrepreneurial frameworks. Figure 4.3 describes the detailed picture of BRICS nations for their performance across different parameters of EFC. All the countries are highly focused towards physical infrastructure. Except Brazil, all the BRICS nations have bagged maximum score in physical infrastructure. Amongst all the BRICS nations, India is leading in government policy: support and relevance, followed by commercial and legal infrastructure, internal market burdens or entry regulations and entrepreneurship education at school stage.

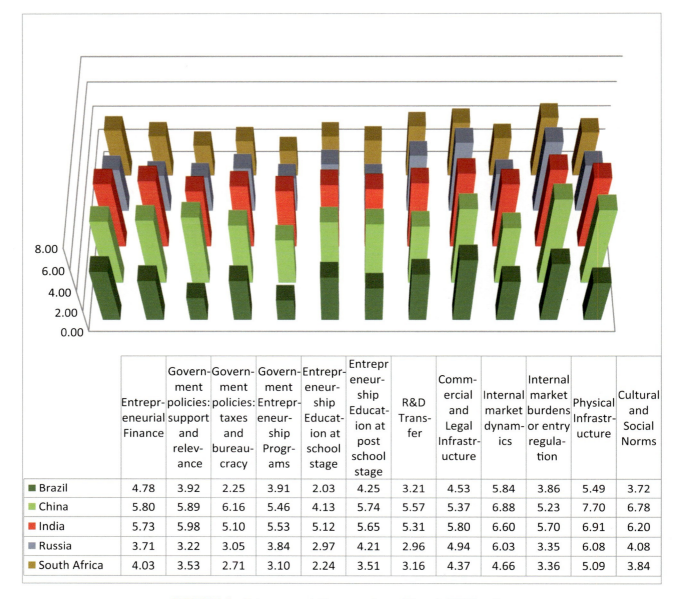

	Entrepr-eneurial Finance	Govern-ment policies: support and relev-ance	Govern-ment policies: taxes and bureau-cracy	Govern-ment Entrepr-eneur-ship Progr-ams	Entrepr-eneur-ship Educat-ion at school stage	Entrepr-eneur-ship Educat-ion at post school stage	R&D Trans-fer	Comm-ercial and Legal Infrastr-ucture	Internal market dynam-ics	Internal market burdens or entry regula-tion	Physical Infrastr-ucture	Cultural and Social Norms
■ Brazil	4.78	3.92	2.25	3.91	2.03	4.25	3.21	4.53	5.84	3.86	5.49	3.72
■ China	5.80	5.89	6.16	5.46	4.13	5.74	5.57	5.37	6.88	5.23	7.70	6.78
■ India	5.73	5.98	5.10	5.53	5.12	5.65	5.31	5.80	6.60	5.70	6.91	6.20
■ Russia	3.71	3.22	3.05	3.84	2.97	4.21	2.96	4.94	6.03	3.35	6.08	4.08
■ South Africa	4.03	3.53	2.71	3.10	2.24	3.51	3.16	4.37	4.66	3.36	5.09	3.84

FIGURE 4.3   Entrepreneurial framework conditions in BRICS nations
Source: GEM India Survey

China seizes the first rank for National Entrepreneurship Context Index amongst all BRICS nations followed by India. Brazil still needs a lot more efforts when compared to other BRICS nations (Fig. 4.4).

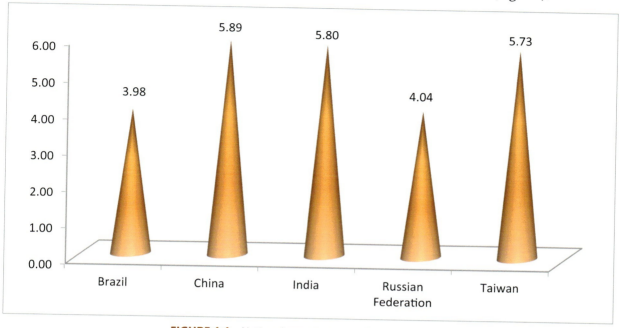

FIGURE 4.4   National entrepreneurship context index
Source: GEM India Survey

ENTREPRENEURIAL FRAMEWORK CONDITIONS, EAST ASIA AND PACIFIC NATIONS

When we compare the performance of East Asian and Pacific Nations, we can observe that India has performed very well across all areas. Again, the comparison is done on the basis of 12 factors, out of which India excels in 3 aspects. India is a leading performer in commercial and legal infrastructure followed by internal market burdens and entrepreneurship education at school stage. In all the nations, governments have majorly focused on physical infrastructure, except Republic of Korea, which is more focused towards internal market dynamics. Entrepreneurship education at school stage demands maximum attention in all East Asian and Pacific nations, except India and Pakistan. Countries like Republic of Korea and Taiwan are doing considerably good but they still lack in entrepreneurial upgradation at school level. On the other hand, India shows an outstanding performance in entrepreneurship education at school stage amongst all the nations. (Fig. 4.5)

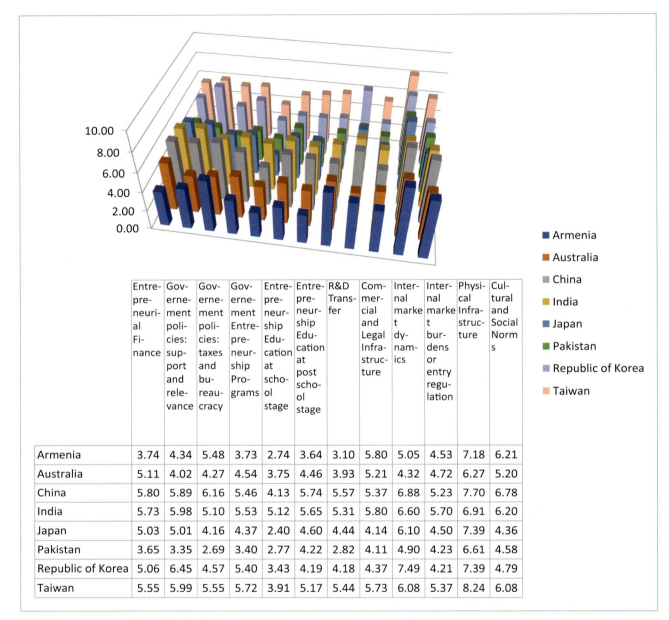

	Entre-pre-neuri-al Fi-nance	Gov-erne-ment poli-cies: sup-port and rele-vance	Gov-erne-ment poli-cies: taxes and bu-reau-cracy	Gov-erne-ment Entre-pre-neur-ship Pro-grams	Entre-pre-neur-ship Edu-cation at scho-ol stage	Entre-pre-neur-ship Edu-cation at post scho-ol stage	R&D Trans-fer	Com-mer-cial and Legal Infra-struc-ture	Inter-nal marke t dy-nam-ics	Inter-nal marke t bur-dens or entry regu-lation	Physi-cal Infra-struc-ture	Cul-tural and Social Norm s
Armenia	3.74	4.34	5.48	3.73	2.74	3.64	3.10	5.80	5.05	4.53	7.18	6.21
Australia	5.11	4.02	4.27	4.54	3.75	4.46	3.93	5.21	4.32	4.72	6.27	5.20
China	5.80	5.89	6.16	5.46	4.13	5.74	5.57	5.37	6.88	5.23	7.70	6.78
India	5.73	5.98	5.10	5.53	5.12	5.65	5.31	5.80	6.60	5.70	6.91	6.20
Japan	5.03	5.01	4.16	4.37	2.40	4.60	4.44	4.14	6.10	4.50	7.39	4.36
Pakistan	3.65	3.35	2.69	3.40	2.77	4.22	2.82	4.11	4.90	4.23	6.61	4.58
Republic of Korea	5.06	6.45	4.57	5.40	3.43	4.19	4.18	4.37	7.49	4.21	7.39	4.79
Taiwan	5.55	5.99	5.55	5.72	3.91	5.17	5.44	5.73	6.08	5.37	8.24	6.08

FIGURE 4.5   Entrepreneurial framework conditions of East Asia and Pacific nations
Source: *GEM India Survey*

Overall, India stands at second position among all the East Asian and Pacific nations after China. Pakistan has a lot of scope for improvement across all the factors except internal market dynamics. (Fig. 4.6)

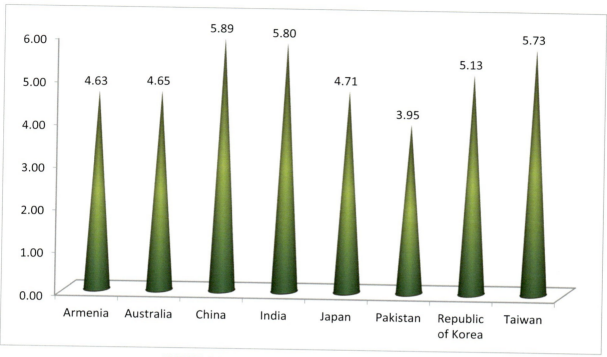

FIGURE 4.6   National entrepreneurship context index
Source: GEM India Survey

EXPERT RATINGS OF THE ENTREPRENEURIAL ECOSYSTEM

India has been ranked 6th for its entrepreneurial ecosystem. According to data of National Entrepreneurship Context Index, India has put noticeable efforts in making physical infrastructure favorable for the entrepreneurial ecosystem. However, the performance of India is appreciable across all the pillars. Figure 4.7 represents the ratings attained by India in various factors of framework. The size of bubbles in the graph represents the ranking attained by the country.

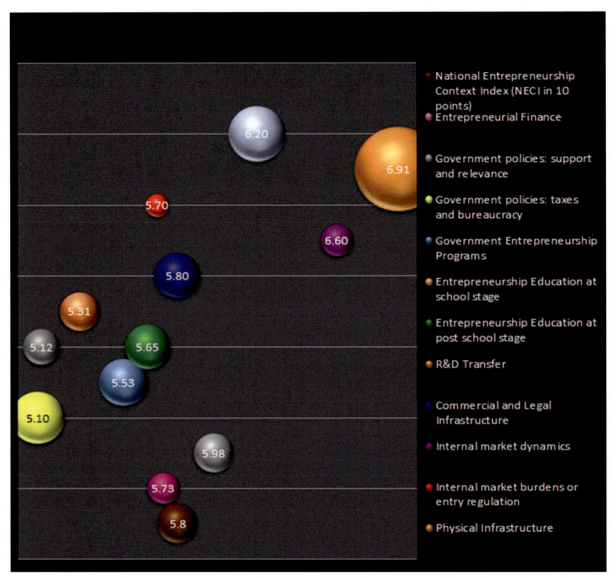

FIGURE 4.7 Expert Ratings of the Entrepreneurial Ecosystem
Source: GEM India Survey, (size of bubble represents the ranking)

ENTREPRENEURSHIP FINANCING IN INDIA

India is ranked 4th among the participating nations. Considering the financial support provided by the government for entrepreneurs, we can observe a tremendous availability of different financial supports for startups and existing businesses. Finance is usually considered the most essential factor for the survival of enterprise. The Indian government is very supportive towards the startup funding. For new as well as the growing businesses, government has supported the entrepreneurs with angel funding, equity and debt funding, IPOs etc. The government also provides subsidies under various schemes for entrepreneurs to start as well as grow their businesses. Further, Government of India has also paid attention towards the growth and survival of informal sector. They also support the informal entrepreneurs to start their ventures and grow them. As per Fig. 4.8 informal sector support bags the maximum value.

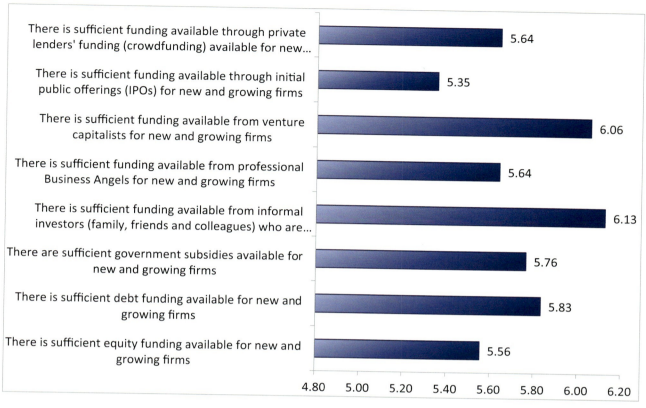

FIGURE 4.8 Entrepreneurship financing in India
Source: *GEM India Survey*

GOVERNMENT SUPPORT AND POLICIES IN INDIA

The ranking of India for government support and policies is 6 out of 54 nations. Government of India has well planned policies and a very efficient mechanism for supporting the existing as well as new firms. The central government of India collaborates with the local government to provide the best support to entrepreneurs. GOI aims to provide support to existing firms in a way that will further help them to grow and survive in the competitive market. Every year government comes up with various new policies. In fact, even the existing policies are reformed as per the current situations at the point of time. However, central government is more actively involved in the support and policy making. In Fig. 4.9 we can clearly observe that local government still needs to put more efforts in supporting the existing as well as new firms.

Further, the Government of India needs to be more supportive towards new enterprises. According to the graph, the government has fewer policies which are particularly for new firms. Many policies are jointly favorable for both existing as well new firms, but, new firms have their own basket of problems. Many such issues cannot be handled by the joint policies. Therefore, it is highly required that government focuses on launch of policies which are particularly for the new firms.

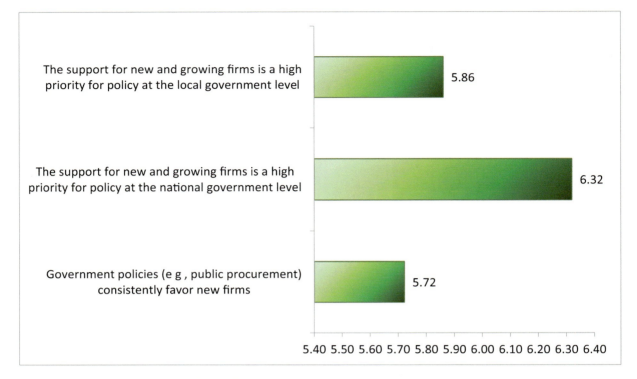

FIGURE 4.9 Government support and policies in India
Source: GEM India Survey

TAXES AND BUREAUCRACY IN INDIA

India is being ranked 11th and as compared to the previous year records, government has improved the taxation and bureaucracy in the country. Across all four factors of tax and bureaucracy we can observe a better value, which indicates a better and improved ecosystem for the new and existing firms. The maximum improvement can be seen in coping with the government bureaucracy, regulations and licensing requirements. In India, the government tax and regulations are very predictable as well as consistent, which is suitable for the firms. This helps them in survival and growth of their firm. Additionally, this improves the ecosystem for the entrepreneurs.

Still a lot more focus is required for the problems faced by new firms. New firm establishment required various permits from the government. In many countries these permits are comparatively easier to get. But in India, still new firms face a lot of issues and require a considerable span of time to get these permits. (Fig. 4.10)

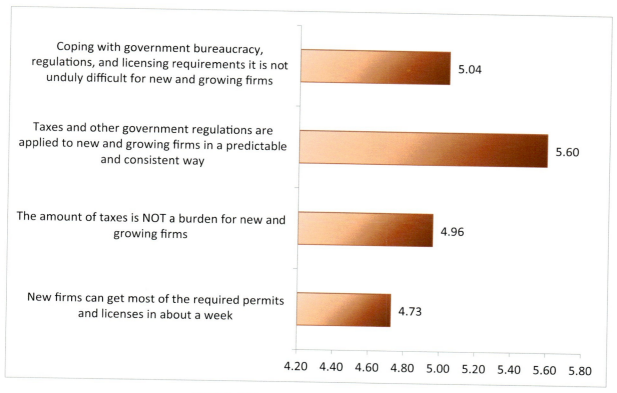

FIGURE 4.10 Taxes and bureaucracy in India
Source: GEM India Survey

GOVERNMENT PROGRAMS IN INDIA

As per the data by GEM survey, government has adequate number of programs to help the new and existing firms. The government of India has invested a good amount on science parks and business incubators, which is very helpful for firms, especially for the new firms and startups. For this, India has bagged 9th rank out of 54 economies that participated in this survey. Figure 4.11 highlights the detailed information about the government programs that support the existing and new businesses through various means. In addition to this, a considerable point is that government is very successful in providing assistance to large number of entrepreneurs through these programs. The GOI needs to focus towards the help and assistance provided by the government agencies. Still, people working at government agencies are not very competent and effective in supporting new and growing firms.

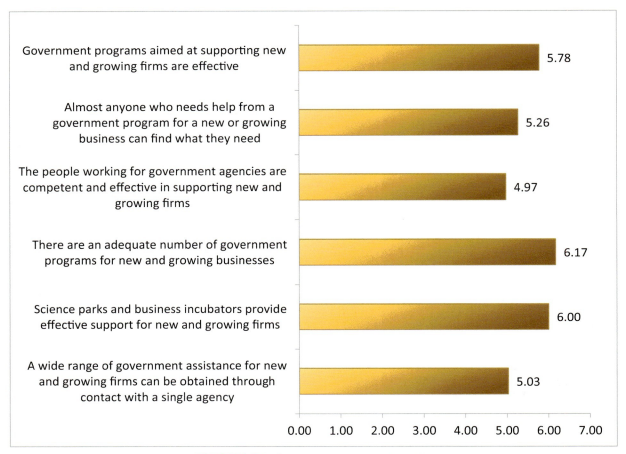

FIGURE 4.11   Government programs in India
Source: *GEM India Survey*

EDUCATION – PRIMARY AND SECONDARY IN INDIA

A lot of focus of government is now shifting towards primary and secondary level of entrepreneurial education. At school level, teachers are engaging children in lot of creative activities which develop entrepreneurial skills among the students at an early stage of life. These activities help the students to cope up with different situations and develop themselves according to the environment. All this contributes later when they have to deal with the dynamic business environments. In this aspect, India stands at number 5 among the participating nations.

But only engaging in these activities is not sufficient. Students need to know enough about entrepreneurship so that they could consider it as a career option. It is very necessary that students get enlightened about the entrepreneurship as their career option in future. For this schools have to teach them about the fundamentals and cores of entrepreneurship. It is important that students get aware about this at school level, both primary as well as secondary. (Fig. 4.12)

As per the data, government needs to put a lot of effort to start educating students about entrepreneurship at school level. Currently, very less effort can be seen towards the entrepreneurial education in schools.

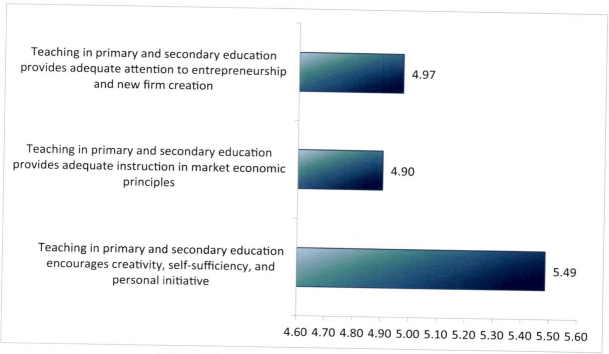

FIGURE 4.12   Education – primary and secondary in India
Source: *GEM India Survey*

EDUCATION – POST-SECONDARY LEVEL IN INDIA

At post-secondary level, government is inculcating many vocational as well as professional courses, which are highly focused on entrepreneurship. Many institutions are being set up which are specialised in the entrepreneurial training among the students. Through these courses, students get proper training to start their own business. This also encourages the youth as well as makes them confident about their ability to run a successful enterprise. India ranks 8th among all the nations for their entrepreneurial education at post-secondary level.

As compared to the previous year, we can observe an increase in such vocational and professional courses in the institutions. Adding to this, there is an increase in the level of preparation for the growth of businesses and startups. There is also marked increase in the adequate preparation required among the students for firms and startups as compared to previous year, but, still a lot of effort is required in this area. The government should encourage the educational institutions so that they can contribute better in preparing the youth for growth of enterprises and startups. (Fig. 4.13)

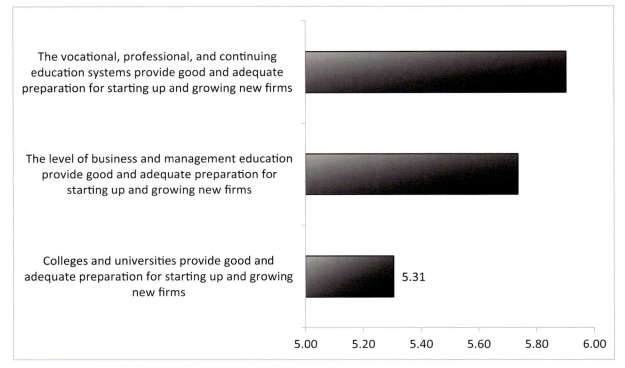

FIGURE 4.13   Education – Post-Secondary level in India
Source: *GEM India Survey*

COMMERCIAL AND LEGAL INFRASTRUCTURE IN INDIA

Compared to previous year, India is able to shift its position from 9th rank to 8th rank this year. Considering the commercial and legal infrastructure, the ecosystem of the country is quite favorable. As per the survey data of GEM, it is easy for existing as well as new firms to get the banking facilities. For any business, banking services are one of the most important services to run a smooth business. If these services get hampered, it gets very difficult for firms to run their operations smoothly. Considering the importance of banking, government has put sufficient efforts to make banking services available to all entrepreneurs. The current strategy of government, making India cashless, helps the entrepreneurs in much larger way. This makes the services just a click away for firms as well as their customers. This accommodates both the parties in the market and supports them for smooth and consistent transactions. (Fig. 4.14)

Another functionality required for a smooth running of a business is the professional and legal help. Businesses have to keep a good record of their transactions and peculiar details of their working. All this is possible when they have experts to help them record their proceedings. This requires the help of professional and legal services as well as accountants. In India, entrepreneurs have an easy access to such services. Further, if considering the subcontractors, suppliers and consultants, entrepreneurs do not find it a hustle, but there is a great scope of improvement. Still, entrepreneurs have to put considerable efforts to get suitable subcontractors, suppliers and consultants.

INTERNAL MARKET DYNAMICS IN INDIA

We can observe a drastic shift in country's ranking this year. The ranking of India is 4th as compared to 7th rank last year. Every year, India is getting better at internal market dynamics. We can observe a consistent improvement, leading towards a favourable ecosystem for the entrepreneurs. As compared to previous year, both business-to-business and consumer goods and services recorded the improvement. Still, there is more scope for improvement in business-to-business goods and services market dynamics. (Fig. 4.15)

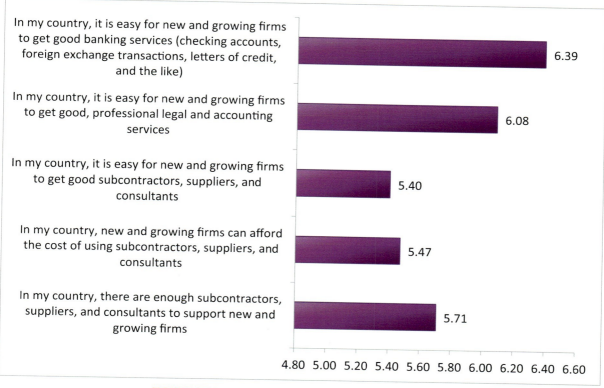

FIGURE 4.14   Commercial and legal infrastructure in India
Source: GEM India Survey

FIGURE 4.15   Internal market dynamics in India
Source: GEM India Survey

INTERNAL MARKET OPENNESS IN INDIA

Again, in internal market openness, India has considerably improved its position from rank 6th to 2nd this year. Compared to previous year, we can observe appreciable improvement in anti-trust legislation. Further, considerable efforts can be seen in the affordability factor of firms to enter the market. Eventually, now it is easier for firms to enter the market. Affordability is not much of a problem, which encourages more startups to establish themselves and enter the competitive market. Other than affordability, overall, the government has focused a lot to make it easier for the firms to enter and sustain in the market. However, there is a lot of scope for improvement when we consider the blockage created by the established firms. New firms are afraid of the big competitors in the market. And this is one of the major factors that stops the new firms to enter the market. Not only the new firms suffer from this blockage, but, some existing smaller firms face a lot of difficulty in growth. If we need a healthy and competitive market, then, government needs to focus on this problem. Otherwise, this can violate the healthy competition of the market. (Fig. 4.16)

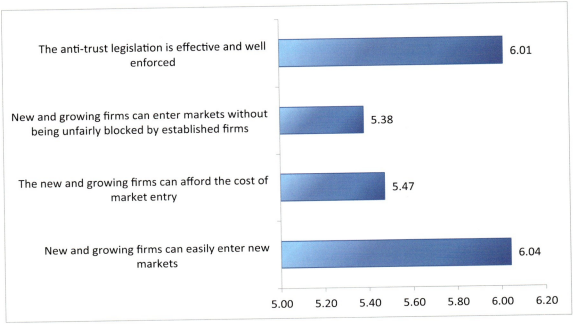

FIGURE 4.16   Internal market openness in India
Source: *GEM India Survey*

PHYSICAL INFRASTRUCTURE IN INDIA

Out of all the 12 factors, physical infrastructure is the most developed and focused area. Physical infrastructure plays a vital role and government has paid sufficient attention on development of the physical infrastructure in the country. As compared to previous year, there is an improvement across all the infrastructural facilities. Especially, there is a noticeable increase in the basic facilities and communicational access (Fig. 4.17). Government has not only focused on the availability, but, also on the affordability factor. For the new firms, affordability of such services is a crucial factor. For existing as well as new and growing firms, it is very affordable to get all the basic infrastructure facilities as well as communication access.

R&D TRANSFER IN INDIA

The R&D transfer has improved when compared to previous year. Specially, the affordability of latest technology for new and growing firms has improved. But, the new and growing firms do not enjoy equal opportunities when it comes to accessibility of new research and technology as compared to large and established firms. The government is very supportive towards the commercialisation aspect of researches done by engineers, scientists and universities. (Fig. 4.18)

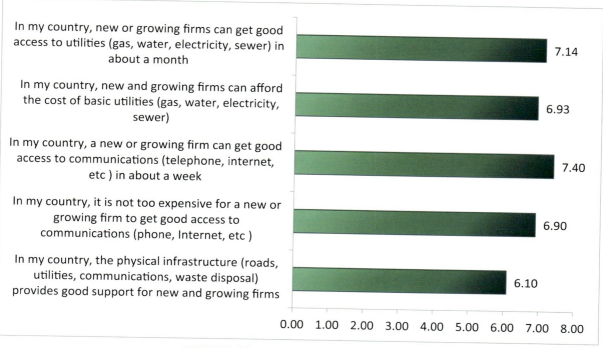

FIGURE 4.17   Physical infrastructure in India
Source: *GEM India Survey*

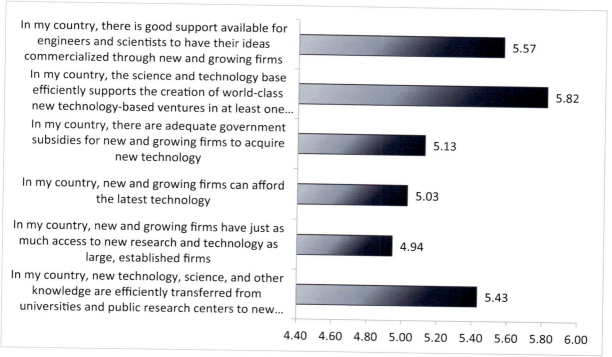

FIGURE 4.18   R&D transfer in India
Source: *GEM India Survey*

CULTURAL AND SOCIAL NORMS IN INDIA

Improving the cultural and social norms, India is ranked 12th this year and has enhanced its ranking by two places as compared to the previous year. Overall, the social and cultural norms are favourable in India. As compared to previous year, a lot of improvement can be observed in all the factors. Figure 4.19 gives detailed information about the contribution of cultural and social norms that encourage the entrepreneurs in setting up a successful enterprise as well as in the growth of these firms. One of the best factors is that, the country's culture and social norms encourage the risk-taking factor, which is a very supportive aspect for any entrepreneur.

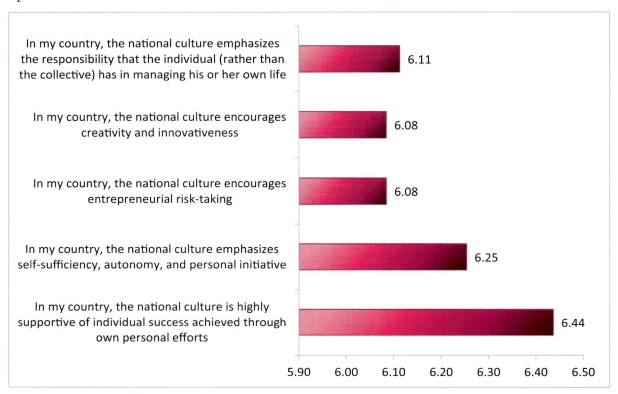

FIGURE 4.19   Cultural and social norms in India
Source: GEM India Survey

CONSTRAINS, FOSTERING FACTORS AND RECOMMENDATIONS TO STRENGTHEN ENTREPRENEURSHIP IN INDIA

According to the NES 2019–20 highlights, 5 factors are considered as the constraints in the entrepreneurial environment of India. These 5 factors include financial support; government policies; cultural and social norms; political, institutional and social context; and economic climate. Figure 4.20 shows the percentage share of constraints in the economy.

Similarly, Fig. 4.21 shows the fostering factors involved in the entrepreneurial ecosystem of India. Government policies, education and training, capacity to entrepreneurs, financial support and access to physical infrastructure contributes as the fostering factors in India. Among these five, government policy bags the maximum share.

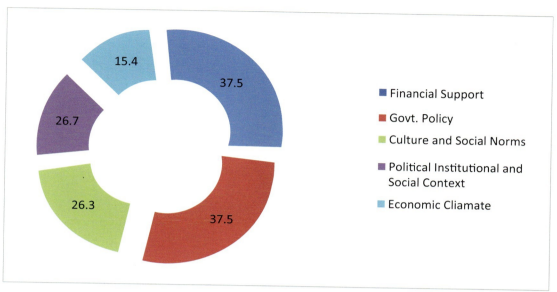

FIGURE 4.20   Constrains of entrepreneurship in India
Source: GEM India Survey, (in percentages)

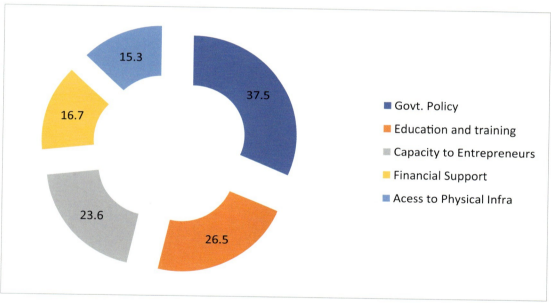

FIGURE 4.21   Fostering factors for entrepreneurial activity in India
Source: GEM India Survey, (in percentages)

Further, Fig. 4.22 highlights the recommendations that can improve entrepreneurial activities in India. As per the data, government needs to focus on the government policies at the most, followed by education and training and financial support. The graph in this figure showcases the share of these three factors that are recommended to improve the entrepreneurial ecosystem in India.

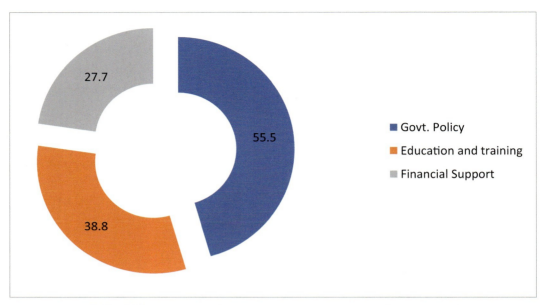

FIGURE 4.22   Recommendations to improve entrepreneurial activity in India
Source: *GEM India Survey, (in percentages)*

5 Conclusion and Policy Suggestions

Global GEM over the last 21 years has grown as a source of great information for entrepreneurial activity, entrepreneurial motivations, perceptions and activities. The 2019–20 survey and data analysis provides a range of new information relevant to the entrepreneurship ecosystem as well. Entrepreneurship growth in the country is clearly visible in this GEM 2019–20 survey. The detailed information is a product of the survey conducted and experts interviewed for this study in India and throughout the world, by global entrepreneurship teams. It is a result of a huge survey, answering the same questionnaire throughout the global entrepreneurship monitored participants.

Every year improvements are made and new additions in the data collection are introduced. In this year too improved questions for motivations of new entrepreneurship are given. It highlights the motivations of a purpose-driven entrepreneurship in different countries and India in particular. The emergence of a purpose-driven entrepreneurship alongside more traditional motivations of generating income or choosing entrepreneurship due to scarcity of jobs are major highlights, in this year's GEM analysis. The data for 2019–20 also improved on self-perceptions of opportunism and proactivity. The questions are improved to understand the actions and probability of taking entrepreneurship as a career. This new information and the entrepreneurial activity in the country can open new research areas and provide more viable data sources.

GEM survey is a country-wide survey of entrepreneurs, adults, nascent entrepreneurs, established entrepreneurs, female entrepreneurs, experts, and start-up-founders to understand the entrepreneurship status and perceptions. GEM data is acknowledged worldwide as the finest source for entrepreneurship information. It has retained an important position with reference to researchers and policymakers to enhance the global outlook of entrepreneurship in a country. GEM data brings together both personal and societal perspectives to entrepreneurship as well as expert views on the ecosystem to analyse and look into the entrepreneurship status of the country. It is a rich source of data for academicians, entrepreneurship researchers, policymakers and professionals who rely on this data and increase their awareness and enhance knowledge base related to entrepreneurship in the country. Also, it is a rich source of information to understand the multilayered dimensions of entrepreneurship in the country.

India is bestowed with the biggest demographic dividend in the world and a good human resource is considered a wealth for the country. Interestingly, India holds nearly 17% of the world population which is young and ready to work. Analysis of APS data has given a strong overview of the current entrepreneurship condition in India and also highlights the areas of concern and areas of improvement to us. Let's discuss the major key points from the 2019–20 GEM India survey.

KEY POINTS FROM THE ADULT POPULATION SURVEY (APS)

❏ There is a strong percentage of respondents who positively answered the 'know someone who has started a new business'. The data highlights that around 64% of the population knows someone who has started a business recently or lately.

❏ The data for percentage of population who perceive there are good opportunities in their area for new business has gained positively from the preceding years. The data shows that 83% of the population perceives that there is a good opportunity to start a business in their area. Of the 50 economies who participated India has ranked 2nd for perceived opportunities. Perceived opportunity was 49.8% in 2018–19. This is a clear indication that opportunity perception has changed and improved in India.

❏ The perceived capability approach has gained over the last year and in 2019–20 data, 85% of the population believes they possess skills and knowledge to start a business. The statistics have greatly improved since last year. The data for 2018–19 highlighted that 52.2% of the population has desirable skills which increased to 85% in this 2019–20 survey.

❑ As likely as perceived opportunities has increased, the data for fear of failure among youth has also increased. The data shows that fear of failure has increased among people. It was 50% of population in 2018 who feared of starting a business and fear of failure has increased to 62% of the population. The data highlights that there is a fear of failure among youth to choose and to be entrepreneurs.

❑ Entrepreneurial intention is a very important part of the survey and highlights the possibility of people getting into business. The level of intentions among population keeps changing and compared to last year survey a persistent change has been observed. Entrepreneurial intentions had been 20.6% in 2018–19 and changed over to 33.3% in 2019–20. The big change of perception may be due to the numerous new initiatives that government has been taking and the improved ranking of India in ease of doing business.

❑ The data has greatly improved for easy to start a business in India. The data for 2019–20 reflects that 80% of the population in India considers that it is easy to start a business in India. India has greatly improved in ranking for ease of doing business in the world. There are many other factors responsible for it as well.

❑ The rate of total early-stage entrepreneurship (TEA) in India has also improved and in 2019–20 data, it is clear that TEA in adults has increased to 15% among adults and India now ranks 13th among 50 countries surveyed. Total early stage entrepreneurial activity benefits growth of the entrepreneurship development in the country.

❑ Among female adults TEA has increased significantly as 12% of the total female population is engaged in entrepreneurship in India and 17% of the males are engaged in the same. The male-female difference still exits and needs to be worked on to improve female representation in the overall TEA of the country.

❑ The discussion for established business ownership is important and it is 11.9% of population which is engaged in established business. The numbers decreased to 9.1% for female and 14.6% for male population in the country.

❑ Another important data to discuss is regarding the entrepreneurial employee activity for which India is ranked at 47 and only 0.2% of the survey respondents. The data points are zero for female and it is 0.3 for male respondents.

❑ The data of motivation for entrepreneurship is now more refined and very relevant to the entrepreneurship development in the country. People are majorly motivated by four different reasons to start a business. 86% of the people in India want to start a business to make a difference in the world. The percentage is higher for females and it is 85% males in the population. Another important category is to build a great wealth from the business and data shows 87% of the population is motivated by this. 83% females and 90% of males are motivated by the same objective of building a great wealth.

❑ Among people 79% are motivated because they want to continue their family tradition and this comprises 81% of females and 78% of males. In India, people are also motivated by to earn a living and 87% population wants to pursue entrepreneurship because of this. There is 84% of females and 89% of males in the country who want to start a business to earn a living.

KEY TAKES FROM NES 2019-20

The national expert survey is the second essential survey conducted by GEM every year and this year it was conducted in 54 economies and results are summed up in a newly formed National Entrepreneurship Context Index (NECI). NECI identifies the capacity of the ecosystem of the particular country for the enhancement of the entrepreneurship in the country.

NES survey in India is based on 72 individual experts from field of entrepreneurship, start-up, and academics. Experts from various fields directly or indirectly involved with the entrepreneurship domain, suggest new things towards the improvement of the entrepreneurship framework conditions. However, the experts feel that the following constraints still hinder growth of entrepreneurship and development in India. Among the NES experts, 37% perceive financial support as a major constraint for the strengthening of the entrepreneurship ecosystem of the country. Finance has been highlighted by a number of researchers as an important constraint for the business start-up and growth in India as well as East Asia. Experts also consider government policy framing and implementation as an important aspect for the development of entrepreneurship in the country. Experts also consider cultural and social norms, political institutions and social context, and economic climate as important constraints for entrepreneurship growth in the country. (Fig. 5.1)

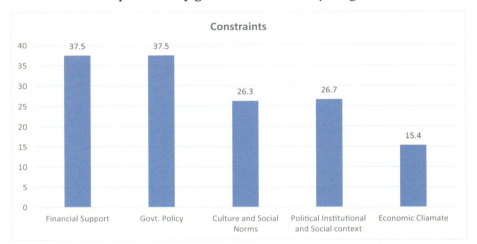

FIGURE 5.1   Important constraints for entrepreneurship growth in the country
Source: *NES India Survey*

At the same time, the major enablers for entrepreneurship development in India are as follows. Figure 5.2 provides enablers for entrepreneurship in the country. The experts highlight government policies their formulation and implementation as important enablers. Another 26% of the experts highlight that education and training are vital in enabling entrepreneurship in the country. While 23% experts believe that capacity to entrepreneurs, 16% of experts believe greater financial support and 15% believe access to physical infrastructure are great enablers to entrepreneurship in the country.

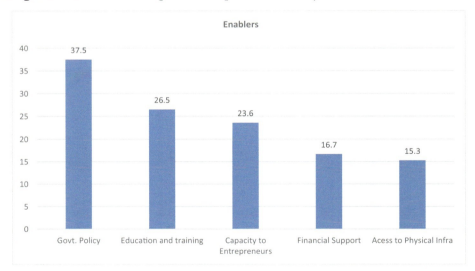

FIGURE 5.2   Enablers for entrepreneurship in the country
Source: *NES India survey*

Experts have also given their suggestion and recommendation for improving overall entrepreneurial ecosystem of the country. The three major points given by experts are to improve **government policy** and its implementation regarding entrepreneurship development. Introduce and increase **entrepreneurship education** in the country and increase **financial support** and its reimbursement to the intended entrepreneurs in the country.

ENTREPRENEURSHIP POLICY RECOMMENDATIONS FOR INDIA

The demographic dividend of India is a deciding factor in the future of the country. Entrepreneurship is being promoted with utmost enthusiasm and policy makers hope that entrepreneurship is the future of the country. The number of start-up unicorns has been increasing and adding to the list. The easiest way to set a thing into the minds is done through its students. The change in the mindset and positive thoughts for entrepreneurship will lead to a greater entrepreneurial activity. A culture of entrepreneurship will boost the entrepreneurship automatically.

Entrepreneurship education at both secondary and higher levels needs policy attention. The changes in the way that only few boards have included entrepreneurship in the curriculum opens way to higher education institutions to introduce entrepreneurship as a part of their curriculum to foster entrepreneurship in the country.

Looking at the NES data, it is clear that ecosystem is growing but experts look concerned about many of the framework conditions. As 0 in the Likert scale indicates very inadequate and insufficient, and 10 as most adequate, majority of the final expert rankings are between 5 and 6. Only internal market dynamics, physical infrastructure, cultural and social norms surpass the limit of five (neither good nor bad) in a scale of 0–10. This indicates a need for greater encouragement and boosting of entrepreneurial activity in the country. However, with new initiatives by the government this tends to be improving. Overall, the expert survey indicates positively towards the existing and improving entrepreneurial ecosystem in the country. Also, with the new initiatives by the government, there is bound to be further improvement in the coming years.

Concluding this assessment of perceptions and expert opinions for a country of more than a billion population, with many billionaires as well as critical poverty zones, is not easy. However, it is inevitable to say that the government and private organisations play a great role in making India, already the third largest entrepreneurship ecosystem, a more significant global market driven by innovation, human capital, skilled labour, entrepreneurial ventures and funding agencies.

Entrepreneurship Development Institute of India, Ahmedabad

The Entrepreneurship Development Institute of India (EDII), Ahmedabad was set up in 1983 as an autonomous and not-for-profit institute with support of apex financial institutions - the IDBI Bank Ltd., IFCI Ltd., ICICI Bank Ltd. and State Bank of India (SBI). The Government of Gujarat pledged twenty-three acres of land on which stands the majestic and sprawling EDII Campus. EDII began by conceptualising Entrepreneurship Development Programmes (EDPs), and subsequently launched a fine tuned and tested training model for New Enterprise Creation, popularly known as EDII-EDP model. Gradually, EDII moved on to adopt the role of a National Resource Institute in the field, broad basing its efforts internationally too, with the setting up of Entrepreneurship Development Centres in Cambodia, Laos, Myanmar, Vietnam and Uzbekistan. EDII works with the central government and various state governments in a collaborative frame. The institute plays a major role in creating and sharpening the entrepreneurial culture in Gujarat and the country.

It conducts a variety of programmes and projects across sectors under its in-house Departments of Policy Advocacy, Knowledge and Research, Entrepreneurship Education; Projects; Business Development Services & National Outreach and Developing Economy Engagement. Emphasizing on research, EDII also set up the Centre for Research in Entrepreneurship Education and Development (CREED) on its campus, in the year 1997. The goal of CREED is to facilitate expansion of the boundaries of knowledge and give an identifiable thrust to the entrepreneurship development movement. The focus areas of CREED include Entrepreneurship Education, Innovations in Training Techniques, Voluntary Sector: Issues and Interventions, Gender and Enterprise Development, Micro Finance and Micro Enterprise Development and Emerging Profile of Entrepreneurship.

In consonance with the emphasis on start-ups and innovations, EDII has hosted the Technology Business Incubator (TBI), CrAdLE. The TBI is catalysed and supported by DST, Govt. of India. It focusses on incubating start-ups in the potential areas of food/agriculture, manufacturing, renewable energy and healthcare.

The first national resource institute in entrepreneurship training, research, education and institution building, EDII has successfully brought about a change in the way entrepreneurship is perceived. The institute has earned regional, national and international recognition for boosting entrepreneurship and start-ups across segments and sectors through innovative models and by intermediating creatively among stakeholders such as; new age potential entrepreneurs, existing entrepreneurs, incubation centres, and venture capitalists.

THE DEPARTMENTS AT EDII

Policy Advocacy, Knowledge and Research

An acknowledged Centre for Research in Entrepreneurship, Public Policy & Advocacy, this department seeks to provide conceptual underpinnings to national and international policies, assist policy makers in their efforts to promote entrepreneurship opportunities and call upon government bodies and private organizations to integrate entrepreneurship in their development policies.

Entrepreneurship Education

To augment the supply of new entrepreneurs, this department aims at establishing entrepreneurship as an academic discipline and creating a conducive ecosystem for its growth. The department offers industry relevant approved academic courses and programmes to strengthen entrepreneurship education, and undertakes curriculum development on entrepreneurship, thus establishing higher-order achievements in the domain.

Department of Projects

Towards undertaking projects for economic and entrepreneurial transformations, this department works for the corporates as well as the government. It aims at partnering with government to implement innovation-led projects, institutionalising S & T entrepreneurship in academic and specialised institutions, developing and enhancing skills of potential/existing entrepreneurs in emerging sectors such as agriculture, food processing, handlooms, tourism, etc. and collaborating with corporates to build intrapreneurial skills.

Business Development Services and National Outreach

Considering the significance of fostering global competitiveness and growth of Micro, Small & Medium Enterprises (MSMEs), this department targets providing business development services across regions and sectors, accelerating start-ups, facilitating growth of existing MSMEs and catering to the requirements of MSMEs across the country.

Developing Economy Engagement

In order to facilitate developing countries to establish a flourishing entrepreneurial eco-system, this department aims at institutionalising entrepreneurship development initiatives in developing countries, sensitising stakeholders in the entrepreneurial ecosystem in the developing economies about the ways and means of promoting and sustaining MSMEs and training and skilling to ensure human resource development.

Appendix

1. Entrepreneurial Activity, GEM 2019 – Percentage of opulation Aged 18–64

Economy	Region	Average Income Level	Nascent Entrepreneurship Rate Score	Rank/50	New Business Ownership Rate Score	Rank/50	Early-stage Entrepreneurial Activity (TEA) Score	Rank/50	Established Business Ownership (EBO) Rate Score	Rank/50	Employee Entrepreneurial Activity (EEA) Score	Rank/50
Armenia	East Asia & Pacific	Middle	14.1	5	7.4	10	21.0	7	7.8	23	0.6	38T
Australia	East Asia & Pacific	High	5.8	30	5.1	17	10.5	27T	6.5	29	8.3	1
Belarus	Europe and North America	Middle	3.0	46	2.8	43	5.8	46	2.7	46	0.5	42T
Brazil	Latin America & Caribbean	Middle	8.1	19	15.8	1	23.3	4	16.2	2	0.6	38T
Canada	Europe and North America	High	10.8	10	8.0	8	18.2	9	7.4	24	5.4	13T
Chile	Latin America & Caribbean	High	26.9	1T	11.0	4	36.7	1	10.6	14T	3.6	18T
China	East Asia & Pacific	Middle	5.3	34T	3.6	33T	8.7	35	9.3	18	0.2	47T
Colombia	Latin America & Caribbean	High	15.3	4	7.3	11	22.3	6	4.3	42	0.9	35
Croatia	Europe and North America	High	7.0	25	3.5	36T	10.5	27T	3.6	43	5.9	11
Cyprus	Europe and North America	High	7.9	20	4.6	21	12.2	23	10.1	17	6.2	9
Ecuador	Latin America & Caribbean	Middle	26.9	1T	10.8	5	36.2	2	14.7	4	1.3	33
Egypt	Middle East & Africa	Low	5.0	37	1.8	48T	6.7	43	1.5	49	0.2	47T
Germany	Europe and North America	High	5.3	34T	2.6	44	7.6	41	5.2	35	6.3	8
Greece	Europe and North America	High	4.6	39T	3.8	29T	8.2	39	14.3	5	1.9	26T
Guatemala	Latin America & Caribbean	Middle	11.2	8	14.6	2	25.1	3	14.8	3	1.4	31T
India	East Asia & Pacific	Low	9.4	14	5.9	14T	15.0	13	11.9	10	0.2	47T
Iran	Middle East & Africa	Middle	6.9	26T	4.1	27T	10.7	26	10.2	16	2.0	25
Ireland	Europe and North America	High	8.4	17T	4.3	23T	12.4	22	6.6	27T	7.5	4
Israel	Middle East & Africa	High	8.8	16	4.2	25T	12.7	21	5.5	33	5.8	12
Italy	Europe and North America	High	1.2	49	1.6	50	2.8	50	4.7	38T	0.7	36T
Japan	East Asia & Pacific	High	3.3	45	2.1	47	5.4	47T	7.0	25T	1.9	26T
Jordan	Middle East & Africa	Middle	5.7	31	3.5	36T	9.1	34	6.6	27T	0.7	36T

Economy	Region	Average Income Level	Nascent Entrepreneurship Rate		New Business Ownership Rate		Early-stage Entrepreneurial Activity (TEA)		Established Business Ownership (EBO) Rate		Employee Entrepreneurial Activity (EEA)	
			Score	Rank/50	Score	Rank/50	Score	Rank/50	Score	Rank/50	Score	Rank/50
Latvia	Europe and North America	High	10.5	11	5.3	16	15.4	12	12.9	7	4.3	16
Luxembourg	Europe and North America	High	7.2	23	3.4	38T	10.2	30	4.7	38T	6.7	6
Madagascar	Middle East & Africa	Low	8.4	17T	11.4	3	19.5	8	20.2	1	0.6	38T
Mexico	Latin America & Caribbean	Middle	9.8	12T	3.4	38T	13.0	19	1.8	48	0.2	47T
Morocco	Middle East & Africa	Low	7.3	21T	4.4	22	11.4	24	7.9	22	0.3	46
Netherlands	Europe and North America	High	5.6	32	4.8	19T	10.4	29	10.8	13	6.0	10
North Macedonia	Europe and North America	Middle	2.1	48	4.3	23T	6.2	44T	8.0	21	1.6	30
Norway	Europe and North America	High	4.9	38	3.6	33T	8.4	36T	5.6	32	2.6	22
Oman	Middle East & Africa	High	3.9	42	3.1	41T	6.9	42	2.0	47	1.2	34
Pakistan	East Asia & Pacific	Low	1.1	50	2.5	45	3.7	49	4.7	38T	0.5	42T
Panama	Latin America & Caribbean	High	15.5	3	7.5	9	22.7	5	4.7	38T	0.4	44T
Poland	Europe and North America	High	3.6	43T	1.8	48T	5.4	47T	12.8	8T	1.7	28T
Portugal	Europe and North America	High	6.9	26T	6.0	13	12.9	20	11.0	12	4.1	17
Puerto Rico	Latin America & Caribbean	High	11.3	7	2.2	46	13.4	17	1.3	50	2.1	24
Qatar	Middle East & Africa	High	10.9	9	4.1	27T	14.7	15	3.0	45	3.6	18T
Republic of Korea	East Asia & Pacific	High	7.1	24	8.2	7	14.9	14	13.0	6	1.4	31T
Russian Federation	Europe and North America	Middle	4.6	39T	4.8	19T	9.3	32T	5.1	36	0.6	38T
Saudi Arabia	Middle East & Africa	High	5.4	33	8.6	6	14.0	16	5.4	34	3.2	20
Slovak Republic	Europe and North America	High	9.2	15	4.2	25T	13.3	18	5.9	31	3.1	21
Slovenia	Europe and North America	High	4.4	41	3.6	33T	7.8	40	8.5	19	7.0	5
South Africa	Middle East & Africa	Middle	7.3	21T	3.7	31T	10.8	25	3.5	44	0.4	44T
Spain	Europe and North America	High	2.4	47	3.8	29T	6.2	44T	6.3	30	1.7	28T
Sweden	Europe and North America	High	5.1	36	3.3	40	8.3	38	4.9	37	5.2	15
Switzerland	Europe and North America	High	6.2	29	3.7	31T	9.8	31	11.6	11	5.4	13T
Taiwan	East Asia & Pacific	High	3.6	43T	4.9	18	8.4	36T	12.8	8T	2.3	23
United Arab Emirates	Middle East & Africa	High	9.8	12T	7.1	12	16.4	11	7.0	25T	8.2	2
United Kingdom	Europe and North America	High	6.5	28	3.1	41T	9.3	32T	8.2	20	8.1	3
United States	Europe and North America	High	11.8	6	5.9	14T	17.4	10	10.6	14T	6.5	7

2. Attitudes and Perceptions, GEM 2019 – Percentage of Population Aged 18–64

Economy	Personally know an entrepreneur		Perceived opportunities		Perceived ease of starting a business		Perceived capabilities		Fear of failure, % of 18-64 seeing opportunities		Rarely sees business opportunities		Even when you spot a profitable opportunity, you rarely act on it		Other people think you are highly innovative		Every decision you make is part of your long-term career plan	
	Score	Rank/50	Score	Rank/50	Score	Rank/50	Score	Rank/50	Score	Rank/50	Score	Rank/50	Score	Rank/50	Score	Rank/50	Score	Rank/50
Armenia	55.6	20	53.9	22	49.2	24	70.0	12	48.2	10T	58.4	10	59.4	11T	71.9	3	67.4	22
Australia	55.9	18	45.7	36	66.8	10	56.0	30	47.4	13	38.6	41	63.7	6	52.2	27	65.0	25T
Belarus	50.4	32	29.5	49	35.9	38	42.3	44	38.0	35	39.3	39T	49.1	35	48.0	36	32.7	48
Brazil	51.6	27	46.4	34	39.4	30	62.0	20	35.6	38	58.0	12	54.6	25	63.7	14	85.4	2
Canada	55.1	22T	67.1	12	68.0	9	56.8	28	47.2	14T	39.4	38	59.4	11T	51.5	29T	58.0	33
Chile	71.0	4	47.6	30T	32.9	41	75.5	5T	58.1	2	46.4	27	47.7	38	61.5	17	77.6	8
China	66.2	7T	74.9	5	36.2	35	67.4	14	44.7	21	50.1	23	48.2	36	48.5	35	69.9	19
Colombia	66.5	6	46.7	33	36.0	37	72.4	9	32.7	42	45.5	30T	44.6	43	74.4	1	79.2	6
Croatia	66.2	7T	55.7	21	33.8	40	71.2	10	50.7	8	53.9	16	56.7	20	47.2	37T	65.6	24
Cyprus	56.0	17	38.5	44	38.2	32	58.2	25	36.4	36	32.6	47	33.2	48	45.9	39	57.3	34
Ecuador	59.2	15	55.9	20	55.3	19	78.3	3	35.1	39T	45.9	28T	45.1	41	60.4	20	67.2	23
Egypt	52.0	26	73.5	7	64.0	14	67.3	15	54.8	4	67.8	4	71.0	2	63.6	15	80.5	4
Germany	46.4	37T	52.2	25	47.6	25	45.8	42	29.7	46	45.9	28T	47.8	37	49.7	33	48.6	41
Greece	30.1	48	49.9	28	46.9	26	51.6	35	40.6	33	66.0	6	51.2	33	48.6	34	77.2	9
Guatemala	68.4	5	67.3	10	46.6	27	77.4	4	39.6	34	63.0	7	77.0	1	73.0	2	94.5	1
India	64.4	10	83.1	2	80.0	5	85.2	1	62.4	1	71.6	2	66.2	4	70.3	5	77.8	7
Iran	55.1	21T	47.7	29	30.1	45	68.9	13	36.2	37	48.6	25	46.1	39	66.6	8	63.4	28
Ireland	55.8	19	50.2	27	41.8	28	42.0	45T	31.4	43	36.7	42	25.5	50	22.4	49	23.4	50
Israel	72.6	2	46.0	35	21.6	50	43.3	43	55.4	3	42.2	37	57.7	19	62.1	16	48.9	39
Italy	44.8	42T	45.1	37	74.6	7	48.1	41	27.6	47	25.0	50	27.9	49	24.4	48	26.1	49
Japan	17.1	50	10.6	50	24.3	49	14.0	50	43.5	24	42.9	35	50.4	34	16.8	50	37.1	45T
Jordan	46.5	36	40.6	42	35.1	39	61.7	21	54.4	5	67.6	5	59.4	11T	63.8	13	69.6	20
Latvia	47.0	35	35.6	47	31.8	43	57.0	27	46.6	16	51.2	19	58.3	17	52.0	28	61.3	30
Luxembourg	46.4	37T	58.0	18	60.5	16	48.5	40	45.7	18	45.1	32	58.9	14T	38.6	43	60.9	31
Madagascar	51.0	30	46.8	32	38.0	33	73.5	7	41.0	30	68.7	3	65.0	5	55.5	25	82.6	3
Mexico	46.4	37T	62.8	15	50.9	23	70.7	11	47.7	12	55.0	14	54.0	28	60.6	19	65.0	25T
Morocco	51.2	29	57.7	19	27.0	46	62.4	18	42.5	26	71.7	1	44.0	44	56.2	24	71.6	16

Economy	Personally know an entrepreneur		Perceived opportunities		Perceived ease of starting a business		Perceived capabilities		Fear of failure, % of 18-64 seeing opportunities		Rarely sees business opportunities		Even when you spot a profitable opportunity, you rarely act on it		Other people think you are highly innovative		Every decision you make is part of your long-term career plan	
	Score	Rank/50	Score	Rank/50	Score	Rank/50	Score	Rank/50	Score	Rank/50	Score	Rank/50	Score	Rank/50	Score	Rank/50	Score	Rank/50
Netherlands	51.5	28	64.6	14	84.1	3	41.9	47	27.1	48	28.5	49	42.7	45	43.4	41	41.3	43
North Macedonia	52.4	25	50.5	26	37.2	34	60.9	23	47.2	14T	56.2	13	62.8	7	67.7	7	75.8	11T
Norway	43.3	44	69.5	9	87.4	2	31.5	49	30.2	45	36.0	43	70.2	3	26.7	46	45.8	42
Oman	71.1	3	72.3	8	54.7	20	56.3	29	40.8	31T	51.0	20	54.8	24	56.9	23	70.2	18
Pakistan	44.8	42T	62.3	16	56.4	18	63.0	17	54.2	6	58.3	11	61.0	9T	64.6	11	69.0	21
Panama	45.4	41	53.4	24	57.2	17	72.9	8	40.8	31T	59.6	9	58.7	16	71.5	4	75.8	11T
Poland	50.3	33	87.3	1	90.2	1	50.4	38	45.9	17	45.5	30T	51.8	31	51.5	29T	48.8	40
Portugal	50.7	31	53.5	23	41.1	29	61.4	22	52.6	7	51.3	17T	56.5	22	57.0	22	77.1	10
Puerto Rico	45.7	40	39.4	43	26.5	47	55.7	31	33.2	41	51.3	17T	45.4	40	66.2	10	74.2	14
Qatar	62.4	11	75.6	4	66.6	11	75.5	5T	45.2	19T	50.2	22	53.9	29	66.5	9	79.4	5
Republic of Korea	37.1	46	42.9	39	32.4	42	51.7	34	7.1	50	60.4	8	52.0	30	26.5	47	50.6	37
Russian Federation	57.2	16	29.6	48	31.4	44	35.6	48	45.2	19T	42.3	36	51.3	32	30.2	44	36.7	47
Saudi Arabia	82.6	1	73.8	6	52.9	22	83.0	2	41.8	28	43.4	34	44.9	42	63.9	12	54.3	36
Slovak Republic	65.2	9	36.0	46	25.2	48	53.1	33	43.7	23	49.5	24	58.9	14T	41.8	42	60.0	32
Slovenia	60.4	14	47.6	30T	54.3	21	57.5	26	42.2	27	44.0	33	61.0	9T	58.6	21	64.3	27
South Africa	28.3	49	60.4	17	63.0	15	60.4	24	49.8	9	54.9	15	58.0	18	55.0	26	74.1	15
Spain	42.1	45	36.1	45	38.5	31	50.8	36	48.2	10T	50.9	21	56.3	23	50.9	31	62.1	29
Sweden	54.6	24	79.8	3	78.3	6	50.7	37	42.9	25	30.6	48	56.6	21	47.2	37T	37.1	45T
Switzerland	54.7	23	40.7	41	64.5	13	49.2	39	23.9	49	33.1	46	39.4	46	44.9	40	38.2	44
Taiwan	35.6	47	41.2	40	36.1	36	42.0	45T	31.0	44	35.6	44	38.6	47	28.8	45	50.0	38
United Arab Emirates	61.5	12	66.1	13	66.1	12	62.2	19	41.7	29	47.6	26	54.5	26	60.9	18	74.8	13
United Kingdom	49.1	34	43.8	38	82.4	4	55.2	32	44.5	22	39.3	39T	61.3	8	50.3	32	54.9	35
United States	60.9	13	67.2	11	71.2	8	65.5	16	35.1	39T	35.2	45	54.1	27	69.9	6	70.3	17

3. Gender, Sponsorship & Informal Investment, GEM 2019

Economy	Male TEA, % of Adult Male Population		Female TEA, % of Adult Female Population		Early-stage Entrepreneur with Sponsored Business (Part-owned with employer), % of Adult Population		Early-stage Entrepreneur with Independent Business, % of Adult Population		Informal Investment, % of Adult Population		Median Amount Invested ($US) by those investing in Someone Else's Start-up and saying how much	
	Score	Rank/50	Score	Rank/50	Score	Rank/50	Score	Rank/50	Score	Rank/50	$USD	Rank/50
Armenia	26.0	4T	16.6	8T	5.4	16T	15.6	6	4.4	24	$2,093	34
Australia	12.3	27T	8.8	26	2.5	39T	8.0	20	4.7	19T	$6,913	16
Belarus	6.4	46	5.2	43	1.7	42T	4.1	39T	1.0	49	$2,182	31
Brazil	23.5	7	23.1	3	1.3	45T	22.0	4	3.2	31T	$1,278	39
Canada	21.4	8	15.1	10	9.4	4	8.8	15T	5.4	15T	$7,533	13
Chile	41.1	1	32.4	2	13.6	1	23.1	2	20.9	1	$2,156	32
China	9.4	40	7.9	31	5.1	19T	3.6	42	6.1	8T	$7,225	15
Colombia	23.8	6	20.9	5	6.0	12T	16.2	5	7.7	7	$911	42
Croatia	13.0	26	8.0	30	6.0	12T	4.5	38	2.4	37	$454	47
Cyprus	15.6	18	8.9	25	2.6	38	9.6	12	3.9	27T	$19,050	3
Ecuador	38.8	2	33.6	1	7.3	8	28.9	1	5.5	14	$1,500	38
Egypt	9.2	41	4.1	46	4.9	22T	1.8	49	2.8	36	$598	44
Germany	9.5	39	5.7	41	2.5	39T	5.1	32T	4.6	21T	$7,284	14
Greece	8.8	43	7.6	33	3.2	33T	5.1	32T	4.7	19T	$11,206	7T
Guatemala	28.0	3	22.4	4	2.3	41	22.8	3	14.9	2	$521	46
India	17.1	14	12.7	13	11.6	3	3.4	43	3.0	33T	$574	45
Iran	13.1	25	8.2	29	4.2	26	6.5	26T	5.4	15T	$720	43
Ireland	15.9	17	9.0	24	5.1	19T	7.3	24	4.2	25	$5,603	22T
Israel	15.1	20T	10.4	19	4.9	22T	7.8	22	2.1	39T	$5,618	21
Italy	3.5	50	2.1	49	0.5	50	2.3	47	0.4	50	$16,809	4
Japan	7.8	45	2.9	48	3.3	31T	2.0	48	1.8	42T	$4,625	27
Jordan	11.4	33T	6.8	36T	4.5	25	4.6	37	5.6	12T	$2,116	33
Latvia	19.6	9	11.3	18	3.6	29T	11.9	8	3.9	27T	$3,362	29
Luxembourg	12.0	29	8.3	28	3.2	33T	7.0	25	6.1	8T	$11,206	7T

Economy	Male TEA, % of Adult Male Population		Female TEA, % of Adult Female Population		Early-stage Entrepreneur with Sponsored Business (Part-owned with employer), % of Adult Population		Early-stage Entrepreneur with Independent Business, % of Adult Population		Informal Investment, % of Adult Population		Median Amount Invested ($US) by those investing in Someone Else's Start-up and saying how much	
	Score	Rank/50	Score	Rank/50	Score	Rank/50	Score	Rank/50	Score	Rank/50	$USD	Rank/50
Madagascar	19.3	10	19.6	6	5.9	15	13.6	7	1.8	42T	$104	50
Mexico	13.6	23	12.4	15	7.9	6	5.1	32T	1.4	46T	$1,038	40
Morocco	15.1	20T	7.8	32	7.4	7	4.0	41	2.9	35	$2,600	30
Netherlands	11.5	31T	9.2	23	1.4	44	9.0	13	3.7	30	$5,603	22T
North Macedonia	9.0	42	3.3	47	3.6	29T	2.5	45T	1.7	45	$1,822	36
Norway	11.5	31T	5.1	44T	0.9	49	7.4	23	4.5	23	$5,726	20
Oman	8.1	44	5.8	39T	6.8	9	0.1	50	10.4	4	$5,195	25
Pakistan	5.5	49	1.7	50	1.2	47T	2.5	45T	1.8	42T	$453	48
Panama	26.0	4T	19.3	7	12.6	2	10.1	11	5.9	11	$1,000	41
Poland	5.7	48	5.1	44T	1.3	45T	4.1	39T	3.0	33T	$5,224	24
Portugal	16.1	16	9.9	22	4.0	27	8.9	14	1.9	41	$8,404	11
Puerto Rico	15.5	19	11.5	16	5.0	21	8.4	18	1.4	46T	$1,750	37
Qatar	14.7	22	14.7	11T	6.0	12T	8.7	17	9.6	5	$13,733	6
Republic of Korea	18.3	11T	11.4	17	6.1	11	8.8	15T	2.1	39T	$21,081	1
Russian Federation	10.2	36	8.6	27	2.9	37	6.5	26T	4.6	21T	$1,860	35
Saudi Arabia	13.4	24	14.7	11T	3.1	36	10.9	10	14.3	3	$7,999	12
Slovak Republic	16.4	15	10.2	20T	5.2	18	8.1	19	4.9	18	$6,723	17T
Slovenia	9.9	38	5.6	42	1.7	42T	6.1	29	4.1	26	$8,965	10
South Africa	11.4	33T	10.2	20T	4.9	22T	5.8	31	1.4	46T	$344	49
Spain	6.3	47	6.0	38	1.2	47T	4.9	36	2.3	38	$6,723	17T
Sweden	10.6	35	5.8	39T	3.3	31T	5.0	35	5.6	12T	$4,205	28
Switzerland	12.3	27T	7.3	34	3.9	28	5.9	30	8.9	6	$20,176	2
Taiwan	10.0	37	6.8	36T	5.4	16T	3.0	44	3.8	29	$16,006	5
United Arab Emirates	18.0	13	12.6	14	8.5	5	7.9	21	5.2	17	$9,529	9
United Kingdom	11.7	30	7.0	35	3.2	33T	6.2	28	3.2	31T	$6,272	19
United States	18.3	11T	16.6	8T	6.4	10	11.0	9	6.0	10	$5,000	26

4. The Age Profile of New Entrepreneurs & Business Exits, GEM 2019 – Percentage of Population Aged 18–64

Economy	The Age Profile of Total Early-stage entrepreneurial Activity, % of adult population					Exited a business in past year, % of adult population		Exited a business in past year, business continued, % of adult population		Exited a business in past year, business did not continue, % of adult population		Reason for exit, % of business exits	
	18–24 Score	25–34 Score	35–44 Score	45–54 Score	55–64 Score	Score	Rank/50	Score	Rank/50	Score	Rank/50	Positive	Negative
Armenia	18.4	30.2	20.4	16.3	15.0	6.4	13	2.1	11T	4.3	12T	0.8	5.6
Australia	5.5	13.4	13.5	10.0	8.0	4.5	24	1.3	28T	3.2	20	1.2	3.3
Belarus	6.5	12.3	5.1	3.8	1.1	1.7	47	0.3	49T	1.4	43T	0.2	1.5
Brazil	24.3	26.1	26.7	22.6	12.4	6.1	14	1.4	24T	4.8	10	1.0	5.1
Canada	25.7	29.9	19.1	12.5	7.4	8.4	8	4.7	2	3.6	18	3.3	5.0
Chile	31.6	40.0	43.7	35.2	30.0	8.3	9	1.8	15T	6.6	4T	1.2	7.2
China	10.6	13.1	9.9	7.4	2.8	7.5	10	3.4	5T	4.0	16	1.7	5.8
Colombia	25.0	27.1	21.7	21.4	13.7	5.6	16	1.4	24T	4.2	14T	0.9	4.7
Croatia	13.5	18.0	13.6	5.7	3.2	3.6	29	1.6	19T	2.0	36T	1.1	2.6
Cyprus	10.6	16.8	13.9	9.0	8.3	2.6	41T	1.1	34	1.5	41T	0.4	2.2
Ecuador	30.6	41.9	41.3	32.1	29.9	9.2	4	3.4	5T	5.9	6	1.3	7.9
Egypt	7.9	7.8	7.1	4.8	1.9	8.6	7	1.6	19T	7.0	3	1.2	7.4
Germany	10.1	11.8	7.3	6.3	4.4	3.4	31T	1.2	31T	2.2	35	0.6	2.8
Greece	13.2	6.3	6.5	9.9	6.7	2.5	44	0.5	44T	2.0	36T	0.6	1.9
Guatemala	22.3	32.7	27.0	18.0	13.1	6.0	15	1.7	17T	4.3	12T	0.7	5.2
India	14.6	16.9	15.3	11.9	14.7	5.0	19T	2.1	11T	2.9	22T	1.6	3.4
Iran	9.6	15.4	11.1	7.4	3.2	7.0	11	1.7	17T	5.2	8	0.9	6.1
Ireland	14.2	14.9	12.6	11.6	8.6	4.1	26	1.5	22T	2.5	28T	1.1	2.9
Israel	9.3	16.2	13.8	12.8	9.2	5.3	17	1.5	22T	3.8	17	1.6	3.7
Italy	1.9	7.6	2.7	1.8	0.7	0.8	50	0.3	49T	0.5	50	0.3	0.5
Japan	4.1	7.1	8.0	4.6	2.6	1.1	49	0.5	44T	0.6	49	0.2	0.9
Jordan	5.3	10.4	12.6	8.7	7.8	10.5	3	2.1	11T	8.3	2	0.6	9.9
Latvia	18.9	22.5	19.9	12.2	5.1	3.5	30	0.8	39	2.8	24	0.8	2.7
Luxembourg	7.8	13.4	11.4	12.1	4.0	4.7	23	2.3	9	2.3	33T	1.8	2.9
Madagascar	21.2	21.4	21.1	14.4	12.7	3.4	31T	0.7	40T	2.6	26T	0.8	3.0

The Age Profile of Total Early-stage entrepreneurial Activity, % of adult population

Economy	18–24 Score	25–34 Score	35–44 Score	45–54 Score	55–64 Score	Exited a business in past year, % of adult population		Exited a business in past year, business continued, % of adult population		Exited a business in past year, business did not continue, % of adult population		Reason for exit, % of business exits	
						Score	Rank/50	Score	Rank/50	Score	Rank/50	Positive	Negative
Mexico	12.2	14.1	14.3	12.7	9.3	4.3	25	1.2	31T	3.1	21	0.4	3.0
Morocco	6.5	15.7	15.7	13.4	4.2	2.8	39	0.4	47T	2.4	30T	0.9	3.4
Netherlands	14.2	15.6	11.6	6.7	6.0	2.6	41T	1.0	35	1.6	40	0.2	2.6
North Macedonia	7.0	7.6	7.0	5.5	3.7	3.8	28	1.2	31T	2.6	26T	1.0	1.6
Norway	8.6	9.1	9.2	8.7	6.0	2.6	41T	0.7	40T	1.9	38T	1.1	1.5
Oman	7.2	8.1	6.9	5.6	3.2	15.5	1	4.0	3	11.5	1	2.7	12.8
Pakistan	4.2	3.5	3.3	4.7	1.6	4.9	21T	1.4	24T	3.5	19	0.4	4.5
Panama	22.7	23.7	24.0	23.7	17.1	6.5	12	2.0	14	4.5	11	0.7	5.8
Poland	3.0	11.1	5.2	3.7	2.3	3.2	35	0.7	40T	2.4	30T	0.8	2.4
Portugal	16.7	18.7	14.2	9.4	6.8	3.0	37T	1.6	19T	1.5	41T	0.5	2.5
Puerto Rico	16.1	18.9	17.7	9.5	5.0	2.2	45	0.9	36T	1.3	46	0.7	1.5
Qatar	8.2	15.3	15.3	17.3	19.1	9.1	5	2.5	8	6.6	4T	1.8	7.3
Republic of Korea	4.3	13.4	19.3	15.1	17.9	3.1	36	1.3	28T	1.9	38T	0.4	2.8
Russian Federation	13.1	15.0	10.3	5.2	3.6	3.4	31T	0.9	36T	2.4	30T	0.7	2.7
Saudi Arabia	9.0	11.6	18.5	16.0	10.0	8.9	6	3.8	4	5.1	9	2.4	6.6
Slovak Republic	18.6	18.9	15.9	9.7	4.7	4.0	27	1.3	28T	2.7	25	1.4	2.6
Slovenia	3.6	13.8	9.5	8.6	2.1	1.9	46	0.5	44T	1.4	43T	0.8	1.1
South Africa	8.4	12.6	9.2	14.3	8.5	4.9	21T	0.7	40T	4.2	14T	0.9	4.1
Spain	5.0	8.5	6.9	5.7	4.2	1.6	48	0.4	47T	1.2	47T	0.4	1.2
Sweden	13.2	10.8	8.3	5.9	4.4	5.0	19T	2.6	7	2.3	33T	2.7	2.3
Switzerland	12.1	10.8	9.9	9.1	7.8	3.0	37T	1.8	15T	1.2	47T	1.0	1.9
Taiwan	6.3	11.7	10.9	7.4	4.8	2.7	40	1.4	24T	1.4	43T	0.9	1.8
United Arab Emirates	12.4	16.1	19.8	15.9	11.3	10.6	2	5.0	1	5.5	7	1.3	9.2
United Kingdom	12.2	10.0	10.9	9.8	4.2	3.4	31T	0.9	36T	2.5	28T	1.4	2.0
United States	15.8	22.1	22.1	13.3	13.4	5.1	18	2.2	10	2.9	22T	1.7	3.4

5. Sector Distribution of New Entrepreneurial Activity, GEM 2019 – Percentage of TEA

Economy	Agriculture	Mining	Manufacturing	Transportation	Wholesale/Retail	Infor./Communications Tech.	Finance	Professional Services	Administrative Services	Health, Education, Government and Social Services	Personal/Consumer Services
Armenia	30.5	2.2	9.2	1.1	38.4	2.6	0.9	2.5	1.9	9.4	1.2
Australia	4.8	12.9	6.2	2.8	24.8	6.5	3.0	11.1	6.2	19.0	2.7
Belarus	3.5	7.0	11.0	9.6	31.6	2.0	0.7	6.0	2.0	21.8	4.7
Brazil	0.8	5.3	10.9	5.4	49.0	1.7	0.6	3.3	1.9	16.7	4.4
Canada	5.7	6.1	5.8	2.2	35.6	5.6	5.3	8.0	4.6	13.9	7.2
Chile	5.5	6.6	10.2	5.9	40.5	1.9	1.6	8.5	7.8	10.3	1.1
China	1.7	1.0	6.8	2.7	55.0	2.9	1.5	2.3	4.4	20.3	1.4
Colombia	0.9	2.7	11.3	3.2	55.2	3.0	3.2	4.2	2.9	11.4	2.2
Croatia	10.3	7.4	6.9	3.2	24.7	5.2	5.5	11.6	10.7	13.3	1.1
Cyprus	2.7	6.0	5.7	5.4	34.4	5.5	5.6	8.3	4.6	17.4	4.4
Ecuador	5.6	2.0	6.2	5.0	64.6	2.4	1.5	3.1	1.1	7.1	1.3
Egypt	8.6	6.5	17.0	1.7	58.0	0.0	0.0	2.1	0.6	2.5	2.9
Germany	3.8	2.4	5.7	1.3	20.5	9.6	4.4	9.5	2.7	29.0	11.0
Greece	6.4	3.2	10.1	4.7	42.1	4.1	2.6	6.2	5.2	14.1	1.3
Guatemala	2.4	1.8	13.1	1.8	65.5	3.8	1.2	2.7	1.3	5.3	1.0
India	4.6	3.8	11.9	3.1	61.9	0.4	0.4	1.0	1.4	11.0	0.4
Iran	6.3	6.7	11.1	2.0	28.0	10.2	1.9	10.6	4.3	17.0	2.0
Ireland	4.1	6.7	4.3	2.4	29.2	7.5	3.5	12.7	4.8	20.3	4.4
Israel	0.4	4.2	6.7	2.3	29.9	8.9	3.1	9.7	5.6	25.7	3.5
Italy	8.9	8.5	4.4	3.4	41.2	3.7	1.7	11.8	3.6	11.2	1.5
Japan	7.9	3.9	4.9	6.4	29.1	5.9	4.7	6.7	3.8	24.7	1.9
Jordan	3.0	2.6	9.7	4.2	59.2	0.5	1.3	1.5	1.8	12.8	3.6
Latvia	7.7	6.7	15.8	5.5	24.4	5.6	4.3	9.1	4.9	11.9	4.2
Luxembourg	6.7	7.1	4.5	1.5	21.0	10.1	11.6	13.2	5.2	18.1	1.0
Madagascar	17.5	8.4	12.6	6.2	33.9	0.0	0.0	11.8	2.4	7.1	0.0

Economy	Agriculture	Mining	Manufacturing	Transportation	Wholesale/ Retail	Infor./ Communi- cations Tech.	Finance	Professional Services	Administrative Services	Health, Education, Government and Social Services	Personal/ Consumer Services
Mexico	22.1	4.0	16.1	2.7	51.3	1.3	0.0	0.0	0.0	2.5	0.1
Morocco	1.1	2.0	9.4	2.0	68.6	0.4	0.6	3.4	1.6	8.5	2.3
Netherlands	0.5	3.3	15.8	3.2	59.7	0.2	1.5	0.8	2.5	10.5	1.8
North Macedonia	3.5	5.3	7.9	3.9	21.7	5.9	4.6	10.4	12.6	19.2	5.0
Norway	7.2	8.6	2.6	5.3	19.9	10.0	6.4	12.4	7.2	17.1	3.3
Oman	1.5	7.1	8.5	4.4	44.1	1.0	3.6	3.3	2.9	20.4	3.4
Pakistan	11.7	0.0	14.5	4.0	53.4	0.0	0.0	0.0	2.6	13.8	0.0
Panama	2.7	9.8	9.4	6.0	51.0	1.6	2.5	2.9	3.1	9.6	1.3
Poland	4.7	11.0	8.6	3.5	27.0	2.8	5.4	10.3	3.0	22.1	1.6
Portugal	3.5	5.9	7.4	2.3	35.8	2.0	2.9	12.6	7.7	15.5	4.3
Puerto Rico	3.7	2.8	5.7	2.4	52.3	0.8	0.9	3.2	6.6	18.4	3.2
Qatar	0.8	1.6	5.3	1.8	54.9	2.5	6.4	6.9	10.3	9.0	0.6
Republic of Korea	3.3	3.3	13.5	2.3	48.7	5.7	4.3	3.3	3.7	8.1	3.7
Russian Federation	3.0	6.1	14.9	3.8	41.9	2.4	0.6	3.6	2.7	20.3	0.6
Saudi Arabia	0.9	3.3	5.3	1.1	58.8	1.3	0.5	5.1	2.0	19.9	1.8
Slovak Republic	3.2	8.9	4.5	2.1	20.7	4.5	6.4	12.1	4.5	29.5	3.7
Slovenia	2.5	9.4	14.5	2.5	18.4	6.9	5.8	15.6	5.7	13.2	5.6
South Africa	4.2	4.9	13.1	4.7	46.1	2.9	1.7	1.2	3.9	16.2	1.3
Spain	4.7	3.6	7.3	4.4	29.9	7.3	4.1	17.1	5.1	14.8	1.7
Sweden	8.6	6.7	8.6	2.4	27.3	10.8	1.9	12.5	3.8	14.5	2.8
Switzerland	2.0	0.3	3.4	4.4	21.8	8.4	4.8	12.8	3.8	33.5	4.8
Taiwan	0.5	2.6	11.7	3.5	52.0	4.0	5.0	8.3	1.9	8.9	1.5
United Arab Emirates	0.0	3.0	6.8	3.6	48.5	3.6	4.0	9.8	8.4	10.6	1.6
United Kingdom	0.2	8.8	7.6	0.2	20.4	4.9	3.9	19.7	7.0	23.1	4.2
United States	3.5	6.7	10.5	4.8	24.6	5.4	11.0	11.5	4.0	15.4	2.6

6. The Motivation to Start a Business, GEM 2019

Economy	To make a difference in the world			To build great wealth or very high income			To continue a family tradition			To earn a living because jobs are scarce		
	% of TEA	% of Male TEA	% of Female TEA	% of TEA	% of Male TEA	% of Female TEA	% of TEA	% of Male TEA	% of Female TEA	% of TEA	% of Male TEA	% of Female TEA
Armenia	18.4	17.0	20.3	51.5	53.6	48.7	35.5	38.0	32.1	88.8	87.3	90.9
Australia	51.7	49.4	54.9	64.5	73.6	52.1	22.7	21.5	24.4	41.4	43.9	37.8
Belarus	23.4	18.8	28.3	75.3	72.6	78.5	19.6	23.6	14.9	51.7	46.5	57.5
Brazil	51.4	49.6	53.2	36.9	41.9	31.8	26.6	28.8	24.4	88.4	86.0	90.8
Canada	67.3	64.8	70.7	64.0	64.1	63.9	44.0	45.6	41.6	62.8	62.1	63.8
Chile	44.9	45.3	44.4	40.6	43.4	37.1	25.2	23.7	27.0	68.7	64.1	74.4
China	39.7	36.7	43.9	48.4	54.0	40.8	40.6	33.8	50.0	65.8	64.2	68.0
Colombia	44.4	47.8	40.8	52.5	54.6	50.4	31.7	28.4	35.2	90.1	89.2	91.0
Croatia	35.1	33.9	37.1	49.1	54.6	40.3	35.6	39.1	30.0	74.0	74.7	72.8
Cyprus	45.1	44.4	46.1	73.5	76.8	68.1	30.3	32.5	26.7	58.0	54.8	63.0
Ecuador	52.7	53.4	51.8	36.5	37.5	35.4	35.7	34.7	36.9	82.7	79.6	86.3
Egypt	57.0	54.5	63.0	77.3	77.3	77.4	51.1	54.2	43.7	63.6	58.8	74.9
Germany	44.4	38.0	55.4	32.0	28.9	37.6	68.7	62.1	80.0	42.6	39.2	48.5
Greece	32.3	32.1	32.5	48.2	52.0	43.8	35.3	38.0	32.1	51.6	53.0	49.9
Guatemala	80.2	81.5	78.7	59.8	59.9	59.8	53.2	52.3	54.2	89.7	84.0	96.1
India	86.8	85.7	88.5	87.2	90.1	83.1	79.8	78.9	81.0	87.5	89.9	84.1
Iran	40.6	36.8	46.9	83.5	83.1	84.2	20.9	21.2	20.3	68.7	66.4	72.4
Ireland	26.9	27.8	25.2	28.3	22.3	38.5	69.2	63.8	78.4	40.7	38.3	44.8
Israel	42.7	41.4	44.5	72.4	72.1	72.9	19.2	22.8	14.2	53.9	58.4	47.3
Italy	11.0	6.3	18.6	95.5	100.0	87.8	26.7	33.0	16.2	89.5	85.3	96.5
Japan	43.9	42.7	47.4	48.5	48.5	48.3	32.8	33.0	32.2	32.7	30.3	40.0
Jordan	19.2	18.0	21.4	59.2	55.9	65.0	24.5	25.3	23.0	93.1	92.5	94.2
Latvia	32.5	30.5	36.1	37.9	43.8	27.8	25.6	26.8	23.5	68.3	63.4	76.7
Luxembourg	60.5	64.9	53.8	41.2	43.2	38.1	30.0	28.1	32.9	38.3	38.9	37.4
Madagascar	8.8	11.6	6.3	23.5	25.0	22.1	36.8	38.9	34.8	81.1	79.4	82.7

Economy	To make a difference in the world			To build great wealth or very high income			To continue a family tradition			To earn a living because jobs are scarce		
	% of TEA	% of Male TEA	% of Female TEA	% of TEA	% of Male TEA	% of Female TEA	% of TEA	% of Male TEA	% of Female TEA	% of TEA	% of Male TEA	% of Female TEA
Mexico	65.1	64.7	65.5	51.9	56.8	46.9	48.0	50.6	45.3	85.0	81.3	88.8
Morocco	21.8	21.9	21.4	69.8	72.7	64.3	33.1	32.0	35.0	93.3	92.7	94.5
Netherlands	32.3	27.2	38.7	22.0	29.1	12.9	18.0	20.2	15.2	23.6	17.0	31.9
North Macedonia	56.9	53.4	66.7	53.7	56.5	45.8	68.4	75.5	48.0	83.6	81.0	91.1
Norway	36.6	34.3	42.0	19.5	20.1	18.0	14.5	13.9	15.9	25.6	27.2	21.6
Oman	49.9	38.7	65.9	53.0	49.0	58.7	26.6	29.3	22.7	56.2	50.4	64.7
Pakistan	70.3	63.2	95.1	90.3	87.5	100.0	67.1	70.8	54.5	92.1	89.8	100.0
Panama	76.8	74.5	80.0	64.3	67.0	60.6	52.9	49.1	58.0	86.9	84.9	89.7
Poland	65.4	65.9	64.7	13.3	14.6	11.8	81.6	81.0	82.4	15.8	15.9	15.7
Portugal	41.7	40.1	44.0	43.6	50.7	32.7	31.4	29.7	34.0	54.4	51.4	58.9
Puerto Rico	65.9	66.3	65.4	43.7	43.0	44.4	43.5	45.9	40.5	84.3	81.1	88.2
Qatar	55.5	55.0	57.3	85.3	86.4	80.7	52.1	51.9	52.6	62.2	61.3	66.0
Republic of Korea	9.4	10.7	7.1	67.3	72.4	58.9	5.6	5.2	6.3	35.1	31.7	40.6
Russian Federation	27.1	25.6	28.7	69.7	70.8	68.5	24.9	26.4	23.3	78.8	76.0	81.7
Saudi Arabia	44.6	45.5	43.6	63.1	68.9	56.0	36.4	37.7	34.7	72.4	75.5	68.5
Slovak Republic	40.7	38.8	43.8	33.9	35.0	32.0	28.1	28.2	27.9	63.3	64.0	62.1
Slovenia	48.2	50.7	43.5	47.1	59.3	24.4	23.2	25.8	18.2	60.1	58.3	63.6
South Africa	85.0	82.9	87.1	78.9	83.6	74.0	48.0	43.7	52.5	90.3	89.4	91.2
Spain	49.4	53.8	44.9	59.5	64.8	53.9	13.4	14.5	12.1	42.3	37.8	47.0
Sweden	50.3	50.8	49.3	55.0	61.0	43.8	33.2	37.0	25.9	38.8	41.8	33.0
Switzerland	43.2	41.0	46.9	38.1	46.6	23.5	17.1	20.2	11.8	50.4	47.4	55.4
Taiwan	44.5	40.6	50.4	57.5	61.2	52.1	19.7	18.1	21.9	33.4	30.5	37.7
United Arab Emirates	51.7	50.4	55.9	72.3	72.0	73.4	36.6	37.9	32.2	64.9	62.8	71.4
United Kingdom	49.0	50.8	46.1	51.6	55.9	44.3	5.8	4.6	7.8	64.4	61.3	69.5
United States	66.4	62.5	70.5	69.0	72.8	64.9	30.6	32.0	29.1	41.4	37.8	45.2

7. Expectations and Scope, GEM 2019 – Percentage of Population Aged 18–64

| Economy | Job Creation Expectations | | | | | | At least national scope for its customers and new products or processes | | Global scope for its customers and new products or processes | | Expecting 25% or more of revenue from customers outside own economy | |
| | 0 jobs | | 1 - 5 jobs | | 6 or more jobs | | | | | | | |
	Score	Rank/50	Score	Rank/50	Score	Rank/50	Score	Rank/50	Score	Rank/50	Score	Rank/50
Armenia	7.7	4	6.9	8T	6.4	7	2.5	10T	0.4	25T	4.0	2T
Australia	3.6	24	4.3	21T	2.6	26T	1.7	24T	0.5	16T	1.3	20T
Belarus	2.2	45T	1.9	40T	1.6	38T	0.4	40T	0.1	34T	0.9	26T
Brazil	13.0	1	8.3	6	2.1	31	0.1	48T	0.0	45T	0.1	49T
Canada	9.0	3	5.3	15	3.8	14	3.1	7	0.9	6T	4.2	1
Chile	5.6	12T	17.8	2	13.3	1	2.5	10T	0.4	16T	0.6	33
China	5.4	14	1.6	45T	1.7	36T	0.3	42T	0.1	34T	0.4	40T
Colombia	2.2	45T	12.2	5	7.9	6	1.5	28	0.2	29T	0.9	26T
Croatia	3.5	25T	4.3	21T	2.6	26T	2.5	10T	0.5	16T	2.3	10T
Cyprus	4.2	21T	5.2	16	2.7	24T	4.6	1	0.9	6T	2.2	12
Ecuador	5.7	11	21.8	1	8.6	3T	1.2	32T	0.1	34T	0.7	29T
Egypt	1.9	48	2.3	37T	2.5	28T	0.8	37T	0.1	34T	0.6	32T
Germany	3.3	29T	2.5	34T	1.9	32T	2.0	21	0.9	6T	1.3	20T
Greece	2.7	38T	4.3	21T	1.2	46T	1.3	29T	0.5	16T	1.4	19
Guatemala	6.4	7T	13.2	3	5.5	11	1.2	32T	0.2	29T	0.3	43T
India	6.9	6	6.4	11	1.6	38T	0.3	42T	0.0	45T	0.1	49T
Iran	2.8	37	2.9	32	5.0	13	1.7	24T	0.2	29T	0.5	35T
Ireland	4.1	23	3.3	30	5.1	12	2.5	10T	1.0	2T	2.8	6
Israel	6.4	7T	3.6	26	2.8	22T	2.4	15T	1.0	2T	1.7	16T
Italy	1.0	50	1.4	49T	0.3	50	0.2	44T	0.1	34T	0.4	40T
Japan	2.4	42T	1.5	48	1.5	41T	1.3	29T	0.2	29T	0.5	35T
Jordan	3.2	31T	4.6	19	1.4	44T	0.9	34T	0.1	34T	0.6	32T
Latvia	4.8	16T	5.0	17T	5.6	10	2.2	17T	0.9	6T	2.9	5
Luxembourg	2.7	38T	4.4	20	3.1	20	3.5	4	1.0	2T	2.7	7
Madagascar	12.5	2	5.5	14	1.5	41T	0.1	48T	0.1	34T	0.2	45T

| Economy | Job Creation Expectations | | | | | | At least national scope for its customers and new products or processes | | Global scope for its customers and new products or processes | | Expecting 25% or more of revenue from customers outside own economy | |
| | 0 jobs | | 1 - 5 jobs | | 6 or more jobs | | | | | | | |
	Score	Rank/50	Score	Rank/50	Score	Rank/50	Score	Rank/50	Score	Rank/50	Score	Rank/50
Mexico	3.1	34T	6.9	8T	3.0	21	0.7	39	0.1	34T	0.5	35T
Morocco	3.2	31T	6.7	10	1.5	41T	0.2	44T	0.0	45T	0.2	45T
Netherlands	5.1	15	3.4	29	1.9	32T	1.7	24T	0.5	16T	1.1	24T
North Macedonia	2.7	38T	1.6	45T	1.9	32T	1.3	29T	0.3	27T	1.2	23
Norway	4.3	20	2.2	39	1.9	32T	1.7	24T	0.6	14T	0.7	29T
Oman	3.5	25T	1.8	42T	1.7	36T	0.8	37T	0.0	45T	0.5	35T
Pakistan	1.8	49	1.4	49T	0.5	49	0.2	44T	0.0	45T	0.2	45T
Panama	4.2	21T	12.5	4	5.9	8	3.7	3	0.5	16T	1.3	20T
Poland	2.2	45T	1.8	42T	1.4	44T	0.2	44T	0.1	34T	0.2	45T
Portugal	7.2	5	3.5	27T	2.2	30	2.1	20	0.5	16T	2.4	9
Puerto Rico	2.3	44	7.7	7	3.4	16	2.7	8	1.1	1	2.3	10T
Qatar	4.5	19	1.6	45T	8.6	3T	4.2	2	0.5	16T	1.8	15
Republic of Korea	6.1	9T	5.6	13	3.2	19	1.8	23	0.3	27T	0.5	35T
Russian Federation	2.5	41	3.5	27T	3.3	17T	0.4	40T	0.1	34T	0.3	43T
Saudi Arabia	3.5	25T	1.8	42T	8.6	3T	0.1	48T	0.0	45T	3.6	4
Slovak Republic	5.6	12T	4.3	21T	3.5	15	2.4	15T	0.7	12T	1.9	13T
Slovenia	3.2	31T	3.0	31	1.6	38T	2.2	17T	0.8	11	1.7	16T
South Africa	2.4	42T	5.0	17T	3.3	17T	0.9	34T	0.1	34T	0.9	26T
Spain	2.9	36	2.7	33	0.6	48	0.9	34T	0.2	29T	0.4	40T
Sweden	4.8	16T	2.3	37T	1.2	46T	2.2	17T	0.7	12T	1.9	13T
Switzerland	3.3	29T	3.7	25	2.8	22T	3.2	6	0.5	16T	2.5	8
Taiwan	3.4	28	2.4	36	2.5	28T	2.5	10T	0.6	14T	0.7	29T
United Arab Emirates	3.1	34T	2.5	34T	10.8	2	3.3	5	0.9	6T	4.0	2T
United Kingdom	4.8	16T	1.9	40T	2.7	24T	1.9	22	0.5	16T	1.7	16T
United States	6.1	9T	5.7	12	5.7	9	2.6	9	1.0	2T	1.1	24T

8. National Entrepreneurship Context Index (NECI) and its 12 Components – Scores for 54 Economies

Economy	NECI Score	NECI Rank	Entrepreneurial Finance	Government Policy: Support & relevance	Government Policy: Taxes & bureaucracy	Government Programs for Entrepreneurs	Entrepreneurial Education at School Stage	Entrepreneurial Education at Post-school stage	R & D Transfer	Commercial & Legal Infrastructure	Internal Market Dynamics	Internal Market Burdens	Physical Infrastructure	Cultural and Social Norms
Armenia	4.63	27	3.74	4.34	5.48	3.73	2.74	3.64	3.10	5.80	5.05	4.53	7.18	6.21
Australia	4.65	26	5.11	4.02	4.27	4.54	3.75	4.46	3.93	5.21	4.32	4.72	6.27	5.20
Belarus	4.24	34	3.24	3.28	4.35	3.10	2.63	4.62	3.38	5.26	5.56	4.28	7.40	3.80
Brazil	3.98	43	4.78	3.92	2.25	3.91	2.03	4.25	3.21	4.53	5.84	3.86	5.49	3.72
Bulgaria	4.21	37	4.42	2.54	4.64	2.96	2.69	3.91	3.15	5.13	5.32	4.24	7.60	3.87
Canada	5.16	14	5.28	5.17	4.46	4.70	4.28	5.00	4.23	5.51	5.09	4.84	7.03	6.29
Chile	4.61	28	3.75	4.71	4.79	5.47	2.54	4.93	3.69	4.39	4.13	3.94	7.72	5.27
China	5.89	4	5.80	5.89	6.16	5.46	4.13	5.74	5.57	5.37	6.88	5.23	7.70	6.78
Colombia	4.24	35	3.39	5.00	3.11	4.53	3.05	5.29	3.56	4.02	4.50	3.94	5.76	4.74
Croatia	3.57	50	4.15	3.04	2.46	3.41	2.00	3.28	2.61	3.97	5.51	3.37	6.38	2.63
Cyprus	4.48	31	3.59	4.31	5.00	3.99	3.16	5.09	3.85	5.09	4.41	4.35	6.58	4.41
Ecuador	4.19	39	2.88	3.31	2.66	3.44	3.49	5.39	3.10	4.44	4.99	3.70	6.97	5.92
Egypt	4.33	32	4.54	4.21	3.27	4.12	2.23	3.94	3.07	4.54	5.72	4.48	6.86	5.00
Germany	5.04	16	5.31	4.07	4.15	6.21	2.71	4.80	4.78	6.29	5.79	5.13	6.45	4.78
Greece	4.10	40	3.88	3.56	2.43	3.50	2.62	4.45	4.30	4.92	5.15	4.00	6.06	4.35
Guatemala	3.56	51	2.56	2.39	3.37	2.94	2.75	5.06	2.55	4.43	3.51	3.17	5.53	4.47
India	5.80	6	5.73	5.98	5.10	5.53	5.12	5.65	5.31	5.80	6.60	5.70	6.91	6.20
Indonesia	5.69	8	5.53	5.92	4.98	5.29	4.98	5.98	5.56	5.44	6.57	5.51	6.12	6.37
Iran	3.15	54	3.26	3.07	3.24	3.09	2.98	3.26	3.11	2.98	3.04	3.32	3.50	3.01
Ireland	4.71	24	4.84	4.11	4.50	5.35	3.03	4.65	4.22	4.97	4.84	4.83	5.54	5.66
Israel	4.81	22	5.11	4.06	3.05	4.15	2.98	4.43	4.67	5.62	4.80	4.16	7.09	7.60
Italy	4.31	33	4.50	3.57	3.03	4.13	2.87	4.94	4.64	4.81	4.89	4.51	5.40	4.43
Japan	4.71	25	5.03	5.01	4.16	4.37	2.40	4.60	4.44	4.14	6.10	4.50	7.39	4.36
Jordan	5.24	11	4.90	4.98	3.90	4.50	3.38	5.35	4.99	6.28	6.93	4.36	7.41	5.90
Latvia	4.91	20	4.83	4.37	3.76	5.16	4.18	4.55	4.36	5.87	4.78	5.02	6.94	5.08
Luxembourg	5.17	13	4.31	5.85	5.36	6.00	4.11	5.31	5.31	5.66	3.26	5.17	6.73	4.97
Madagascar	3.69	48	3.00	3.74	3.60	2.92	1.70	5.46	2.93	4.13	4.55	3.38	4.33	4.50
Mexico	4.72	23	4.14	4.04	3.65	4.40	3.12	6.04	4.14	4.75	4.76	4.39	7.08	6.09

Economy	NECI Score	NECI Rank	Entrepreneurial Finance	Government Policy: Support & relevance	Government Policy: Taxes & bureaucracy	Government Programs for Entrepreneurs	Entrepreneurial Education at School Stage	Entrepreneurial Education at Post-school stage	R & D Transfer	Commercial & Legal Infrastructure	Internal Market Dynamics	Internal Market Burdens	Physical Infrastructure	Cultural and Social Norms
Morocco	3.95	45	3.61	3.71	3.84	3.75	2.32	4.13	2.93	4.78	4.82	3.26	6.42	3.82
Netherlands	6.04	2	6.25	5.76	5.49	6.13	5.45	5.84	5.43	6.34	5.29	6.07	7.94	6.54
North Macedonia	3.84	47	3.72	3.12	3.17	3.39	2.83	3.94	3.22	4.85	5.07	3.33	5.83	3.62
Norway	5.52	9	5.49	5.05	4.48	5.43	5.18	5.71	4.66	6.21	5.13	4.80	7.79	6.31
Oman	4.61	29	4.31	4.46	4.15	4.44	3.47	4.40	4.07	4.56	5.56	4.02	6.16	5.71
Pakistan	3.95	46	3.65	3.35	2.69	3.40	2.77	4.22	2.82	4.11	4.90	4.23	6.61	4.58
Panama	3.98	44	3.14	2.59	4.06	4.02	2.08	4.06	2.99	4.30	3.96	3.93	7.21	5.39
Paraguay	3.43	52	2.52	2.41	3.53	3.44	1.88	3.82	2.47	3.44	3.26	3.79	5.75	4.80
Poland	4.24	36	4.94	4.14	2.88	4.30	1.80	3.20	3.53	4.48	6.53	4.07	7.00	3.99
Portugal	4.21	38	4.85	4.26	2.42	4.41	2.63	4.64	3.69	5.00	4.17	3.74	7.12	3.61
Puerto Rico	3.18	53	3.38	2.52	1.20	2.86	1.44	3.73	3.16	3.76	5.07	2.78	4.67	3.55
Qatar	5.91	3	5.40	6.03	6.09	6.05	5.24	6.27	5.21	5.70	5.92	5.09	7.52	6.36
Republic of Korea	5.13	15	5.06	6.45	4.57	5.40	3.43	4.19	4.18	4.37	7.49	4.21	7.39	4.79
Russian Federation	4.04	41	3.71	3.22	3.05	3.84	2.97	4.21	2.96	4.94	6.03	3.35	6.08	4.08
Saudi Arabia	5.04	17	5.01	6.03	5.14	5.32	2.96	4.16	4.09	4.75	5.92	4.74	6.54	5.85
Slovak Republic	4.03	42	4.50	2.82	2.71	3.58	2.67	4.42	2.90	5.09	4.43	4.38	7.43	3.49
Slovenia	4.49	30	4.49	3.97	3.43	5.13	2.80	4.25	3.90	5.13	5.36	4.65	7.06	3.72
South Africa	3.63	49	4.03	3.53	2.71	3.10	2.24	3.51	3.16	4.37	4.66	3.36	5.09	3.84
Spain	5.24	12	4.87	5.33	5.17	5.96	2.65	5.45	5.26	6.04	5.31	5.05	6.95	4.82
Sweden	4.92	19	5.19	3.60	3.51	4.62	4.34	4.84	4.31	5.25	6.07	4.74	7.42	5.21
Switzerland	6.05	1	5.50	5.76	6.21	6.07	4.63	6.33	6.35	6.43	4.49	5.54	8.58	6.68
Taiwan	5.73	7	5.55	5.99	5.55	5.72	3.91	5.17	5.44	5.73	6.08	5.37	8.24	6.08
Thailand	4.99	18	5.05	4.32	4.16	4.25	3.15	4.81	4.26	5.23	6.25	4.67	7.82	5.94
United Arab Emirates	5.84	5	4.91	6.49	5.82	5.94	5.36	5.57	4.72	5.71	6.13	5.13	7.53	6.79
United Kingdom	4.83	21	5.33	4.02	5.08	4.32	3.37	4.65	3.77	5.12	4.85	5.22	6.54	5.72
United States	5.31	10	6.04	4.37	4.90	4.21	3.92	5.42	4.48	5.79	4.99	4.38	7.50	7.68

Bibliography

1. Atal Ranking of Institutions on Innovation Achievements. *About ARIIA*. Ministry of Education, Government of India. https://www.ariia.gov.in/About

2. Bain & Company. (2019). *Powering the Economy With Her: Women Entrepreneurship in India*. https://www.bain.com/contentassets/dd3604b612d84aa48a0b120f0b589532/report_powering_the_economy_with_her_-_women_entrepreneurship_in-india.pdf

3. Department for Promotion of Industry and Internal Trade. *Startup India*. Ministry of Commerce and Industry, Government of India. https://www.startupindia.gov.in/content/sih/en/home-page.html

4. Department for Promotion of Industry and Internal Trade. (2020). *States' Startup Ranking 2019*. Ministry of Commerce and Industry, Government of India. https://www.startupindia.gov.in/content/dam/invest-india/compendium/National_Report_09092020-Final.pdf

5. Department of Economic Affairs. (2020). *Economic Survey 2019-20*. Ministry of Finance, Government of India.
    https://bsmedia.business-standard.com/_media/bs/data/general-file-upload/2020-02/Economic%20Survey%202019-20-1.pdf

6. Entrepreneur India. (2020, January 31). *Economic Survey 2020: New Businesses on a Rise*. https://www.entrepreneur.com/article/345760

7. Indian Institute of Management Bangalore. *Mahatma Gandhi National Fellowship*. Government of India. https://www.iimb.ac.in/iimb-msde-welcome-first-cohort-75-students-mgnf-programme#:~:text=08%20March%202020%2C%20Bengaluru%3A%20The,74%20students%2C%20in%20an%20orientation

8. Invest India. *Andhra Pradesh Ranks #1 in Ease of Doing Business in India*. National Investment Promotion & Facilitation Agency. https://www.investindia.gov.in/state/andhra-pradesh

9. Iqbal Nushaiba and Misra Udit. (2020, September 17). *Ease of Doing Business: How states are ranked, and what's different now*. The Indian Express. https://indianexpress.com/article/explained/ease-of-doing-business-how-states-are-ranked-whats-different-now-6597689/

10. Mukhija Anisha. (2020, January 01). *List of Government Schemes in India*. https://catking.in/list-of-government-schemes-in-india/

11. Ministry of Micro, Small and Medium Enterprises. (2020, February 13). *Shri Nitin Gadkari Flags off Apiary on Wheels*. Press Information Bureau, Government of India. https://www.pib.gov.in/PressReleseDetailm.aspx?PRID=1603054

12. Ministry of Skill Development and Entrepreneurship. (2019, December 09). *Skills Build Platform*. Press Information Bureau, Government of India. https://pib.gov.in/PressReleaseIframePage.aspx?PRID=1595528#:~:text=India%20is%20the%204th%20country,in%20UK%2C%20Germany%20and%20France

13. Ministry of Skill Development and Entrepreneurship. (2020). *Skill India Annual report*. Government of India. https://www.msde.gov.in/sites/default/files/2020-12/Annual%20Report%202019-20%20English.pdf

14. Ministry of Skill Development and Entrepreneurship. (2019, December 19). *Year End Review-2019 of Ministry of Skill development and Entrepreneurship*. https://pib.gov.in/PressReleaseIframePage.aspx?PRID=1596916

15. PRS Legislative Research. *Economic Survey 2019-2020: Report Summary*. https://www.prsindia.org/report-summaries/economic-survey-2019-20

16. Pruthi Rupali. (2020, January 17). *Top 13 Economic Developments: Indian Economy in 2019*. https://www.jagranjosh.com/current-affairs/top-13-economic-developments-how-indian-economy-fared-in-2019-1577793853-1

17. Singh Hemant. (2020, March 31). *Banking Merger in India: Meaning and Benefits*. https://www.jagranjosh.com/general-knowledge/banking-merger-in-india-1567425591-1#:~:text=1.,reducing%20their%20cost%20of%20lending

18. Singh Hemant. (2020, December 01) *International Reports and India's rank in various indexes 2019-2020*. https://www.jagranjosh.com/general-knowledge/indian-ranking-in-different-indexes-1588162961-1

19. Shruthi. (2020, January 13). *Top 20 Sucessful Women Entrepreneurs in India 2020*. https://www.softwaresuggest.com/blog/successful-women-entrepreneurs-in-india-2020/

20. Skill Reporter. *Mahatma Gandhi National Fellowship*. https://www.skillreporter.com/2020/03/news/msde/iimb-and-msde-to-welcome-first-cohort-of-75-students-to-the-mahatma-gandhi-national-fellowship-on-8th-march/

21. The Economic Times. (2019, November 05). *Over 1,300 startups added in 2019, over 8,900 tech-startups in India now: Nasscom*. https://economictimes.indiatimes.com/small-biz/startups/newsbuzz/over-1300-startups-added-in-2019-over-8900-tech-startups-in-india-now-nasscom/articleshow/71925791.cms

22. World Bank Group. (2020). *Doing Business 2020*. http://documents1.worldbank.org/curated/en/688761571934946384/pdf/Doing-Business-2020-Comparing-Business-Regulation-in-190-Economies.pdf

23. National Expert Survey. *Entrepreneurial Framework Conditions*. Global Entrepreneurship Monitor. https://www.gemconsortium.org/wiki/1142

24. About. *Mission and Values*. Global Entrepreneurship Monitor. https://www.gemconsortium.org/about/gem/5

25. GEM. *National Teams*. Global Entrepreneurship Monitor. https://www.gemconsortium.org/about/gem/5

26. GEM. *National Sponsors*. Global Entrepreneurship Monitor. https://www.gemconsortium.org/about/gem/5

27. Gem India. *Gem-India Model*. Global Entrepreneurship Model. https://www.gemindiaconsortium.org/gem_INDIA_model.php

28. GEM India. *NES – Data Collection Process*. Global Entrepreneurship Model. https://www.gemindiaconsortium.org/gem_INDIA_process.php

29. Global Report. (2020, March 3). *Entrepreneurs Worldwide Motivated To Make A Difference. Global Entrepreneurship Monitor*. https://www.gemconsortium.org/reports/latest-global-report